Vogue
Sewing
Quick Reference

sixth&spring
books

Sixth&Spring Books
233 Spring Street, 3rd Fl.
New York, NY 10013

Editor
Crystal McDougald

Editorial Director
Elaine Silverstein

Art Director
Christy Hale

Book Division Manager
Erica Smith

Technical Illustrator
Carol Ruzicka

Associate Editor
Erin Walsh

Cover Art
Lamont O'Neal

Production Manager
David Joinnides

Cover Design
Chi Ling Moy

President and Publisher,
Sixth&Spring Books
Art Joinnides

Vice President, Publisher
Trisha Malcolm

Library of Congress Control Number: 2006932953

ISBN 1-933027-14-2

ISBN-13 978-1-933027-14-2

First Edition
10 9 8 7 6 5 4 3 2 1
Manufactured in China

acknowledgments

Throughout the years, it has taken the contributions of many people to make *Vogue Sewing* as viable as it still is today. We would like to thank them all for their hard work to make this new compendium possible.

Vogue Sewing (2000)
Editorial: JoAnn Pugh-Gannon, Caroline Politi, Stephanie M. Marracco, Nicole Pressly, Beth Baumgartel
Art: Elizabeth Berry, Debra Pantaleo, Jelena Bogavac, Juan Rios, Karen Longato, Greg Kopfer
Cover Photograph: Brian Kraus
Production: David Joinnides, Matt Dojny, Julia Dubrovich
Technical Support: Winnie Hinish and staff, Jim Kingsepp, Ben Ostasiewski, Diane Clark
Technical Advisors: Gail Wheeler, Kathy Marrone, Janet DuBane, Reg Fairchild, Penny Payne, Shirley Asper

Vogue Sewing (1982)
Editorial: Ada Cruz, Hewitt McGraw
Art: Sidney Escowitz, Kathryn Florentz
Production: Hugh MacDonald, Ron Ferguson, Renee Ullman
Staff at Harper & Row: Carol Cohen, Helen Moore, Mary Chadwick

The New Vogue Sewing Book (1980)
Editorial: Elizabeth Rice, Jeanette Weber, Linnea Leedham
Art: Phoebe Gaughan
Production: Maryanne Bannon
Technical Advisors: Margaret Lange, Timothy Healy, Carolyn Galante, Shirley Asper, Robin Harding

The Vogue Sewing Book (1975)
Editorial: Janet DuBane, Elizabeth Musheno, Betty Faden, Ellen Kochansky, Jeanne Johnson, Sheila DiBona, Barbara Trujillo, Caroline Dill, Marion Bartholomew
Art: Tony Serini, Lynne Perrella, Elaine Poprovsky, Dorothy Martin, Janet Lombardo, Susan Frye, Gisela Sachs
Production: Paul Milbauer, Grace Guerrera, Doreen Williams
Technical Advisors: Joe Molko, Alfred Raphael, Leopoldo Hinds, Helen Nemeth

The Vogue Sewing Book (1970, first edition)
Editorial: Patricia Perry, Janet DuBane, Betty Faden, Betty Musheno, Ellen Kochansky, Jeanne Johnson, Gisela Sachs, Sheile DiBona, Susan Frye, Doreen Williams, Grace Guerrera
Art: John Nicodemo, Mel Skriloff, Ed McGloin
Illustration: Dorothy Martin, Janet Grieshaber, Elaine Poprosky, Lynne Perrella
Technical Advisors: Joe Molko, Helen Nemeth
Production: Don Feder, George Keith-Beattie
Marketing and Distribution: Barbara Lolley
Fashion Information Service: Russ Norris, Herman Phynes, Donna Lang

Vogue® *Sewing Quick Reference* has been designed to give sewers the most used sewing information from *Vogue® Sewing* in a compact, portable guide. The perfect size to keep by the sewing machine or slip into a bag for consultation when buying supplies for the next project, this book offers at-a-glance guidance on every step of a sewing project—from choosing the correct size pattern to completing the hem. You will find sections on measuring your body, choosing the correct size pattern, how to find the information on the pattern envelope needed to purchase all supplies for your sewing project, how to use the sewing pattern and individual sewing techniques.

   Vogue Sewing Quick Reference incorporates the best information from *Vogue Sewing* into its concise format. There are the same detailed instructions, clear illustrations and helpful tips. The chapters are color coded for easy reference with each one starting with a colored contents page that lists information and techniques in each chapter.

   Information featured in *Vogue Sewing Quick Reference* was selected to accommodate a wide range of sewing abilities. Techniques for beginning sewers and more advanced sewers have been included, resulting in a collection of information that serves beginning sewers as well as the more experienced sewer. Whether embarking on your first sewing adventure, searching for a creative alternative technique or simply to find the answer to a technical question, *Vogue Sewing Quick Reference* will provide you with thorough information, at a glance, wherever your sewing takes you.

your pattern profile

Accurate measurements are the starting point in selecting your correct pattern size. When taking your measurements, wear properly fitted undergarments plus a leotard, if desired, and your usual shoes so that your posture will be normal. Never measure over an outer garment.

- Make sure the tape measure is held straight and snug, but not tight, against the body.
- Working in front of a full-length mirror, make sure that your tape is parallel to the floor for circumference measurements.
- Tie a piece of narrow elastic around your waist to use as a reference point in taking other measurements. Bend from side to side until it settles in at your natural waistline.
- Stand comfortably, look straight ahead and maintain your normal posture.
- It is easier if a friend can help you as back waist and arm length measurements may be difficult to take alone.
- Double-check your measurements for accuracy.
- Record your measurements with the date.

Review your body measurements periodically so you can be aware of any possible changes in your figure. Even though your weight remains stable, your body contours may shift.

The first four measurements are the keys in determining your pattern size. The remaining measurements will assist you in making any necessary length adjustments.

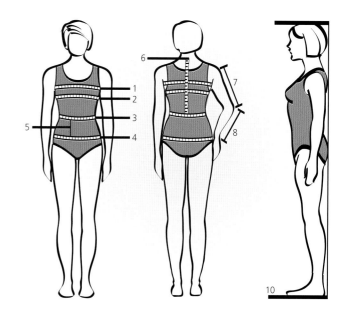

CHEST: Measure around the body, under the arms above the fullest part of the bust (1).

BUST: Measure around the fullest part of the bust, keeping the tape straight across the back (2).

WAIST: Measure around the body, over the elastic (3).

HIPS: Measure around the fullest part of the hip (4) or around the thighs if they are fuller than the hip. The standard distance from the waist to the full hip, called the hip length (5), is 9" (23 cm) for Misses' and Womens' sizes, and 7" (18 cm) for Misses' Petites.

BACK WAIST LENGTH: Measure from the prominent bone at the base of your neck to the elastic at your waistline (6).

ARM LENGTH: With your arm slightly bent, measure from the bone at the top of your arm to your elbow (7) and from your elbow to your wrist bone (8). Adding these measurements gives you your shoulder to wrist bone measurement (9).

HEIGHT: Remove your shoes and stand in your stocking feet against a wall. Standing erect, place a ruler on top of your head, parallel to the floor. Mark its position on the wall and measure the distance to the floor with a tape or yardstick (10).

personal body measurements

Measurement Area	Standard Measurements	Personal Measurements	Adjustments + or -
1 Chest			
2 Bust			
3 Waist			
4 Hip			
5 Hip Length			
6 Back Waist Length			
7 Shoulder to Elbow			
8 Elbow to Wrist			
9 Shoulder to Wrist			
10 Height			

Name:　　　　　　　　**Date:**　　　　**Weight:**　　　　**Pattern Size:**

Standard body measurements can be found in many places, such as the envelope flap, page 1 of the pattern instructions, the back of the pattern catalog and in the Appendix of this book.

Once you have taken your body measurements and recorded them on the chart given here, it is time to select your pattern size. Since almost no one is a perfect pattern match, and it is usually easier to increase or decrease body circumference in the waist and hip area, use your upper body measurements to determine your correct pattern size.

Vogue Patterns are designed for the B cup figure, therefore, it is important to determine your personal cup size. Subtract your chest measurement from your bust measurement. If the difference is:

1" (2.5cm) or less	A cup
1¼" to 2" (3.2 to 5cm)	B cup
2¼" to 3" (5.7 to 7.5cm)	C cup
3¼" to 4" (8.2 to 10cm)	D cup
4¼" (10.7cm) or larger	Larger than a D cup

▶ If you are an "A" or a "B" cup, use your bust measurement to determine your pattern size.

▶ If you are a "C" cup or larger, use your chest measurement to select your pattern size. This ensures a better fit across your shoulders, neckline, chest and upper back. The bust area can be adjusted for a larger cup size if necessary.

▶ If your chest or bust measurement falls between two pattern sizes, your bone structure will be your determining factor. Choose a smaller size if you are small-boned; choose a larger size if you are large-boned.

Because women vary greatly in size and shape, average figure types of varying proportions is the basis for the "grading" or sizing of patterns. Figure type is a matter of proportion, not age. Your pattern is your sewing blueprint, from which you build your exact dimensions for a perfect fit.

Here is where your height comes into play. Misses', Misses' Petites and Women's sizes are designed to allow for your specific height. Shortening or lengthening the pattern is easy to do and will become automatic once your adjustments are determined.

You should also consider the type of garment you are intending to make when selecting a pattern size. For dresses, blouses, tops, jackets, coats and vests, select the size closest to your bust or chest measurement. Adjust the pattern at the waist and hips as necessary.

For skirts, pants, shorts or culottes, choose the pattern size closest to your waist measurement, particularly if there is detailing such as tucks, pleats or darts at the waist area.

If your hips are proportionately larger than your waist—by 13" (33cm) or more—use your hip measurement to select your pattern size.

For coordinates including both tops and bottoms, select your correct size by using your bust or chest measurement.

Now, using the Standard Body Measurement Chart in the back of this book or the back of the pattern catalog, select your pattern size.

understanding ease

Each Vogue Pattern takes into consideration your need for comfort and mobility by building in wearing ease to allow you freedom of movement without restraint. Design ease is an integral part of many styles and will have additional dimensions added to the pattern beyond the wearing ease, as dictated by the garment's design lines.

The pattern caption in the catalogue and on the back of the pattern envelope describes how the garment is intended to fit. Some women prefer loosely fitting clothes while others prefer clothes fitted more closely to the body. Use this information to help you select the type of fit in your garments that is most flattering to your figure.

wearing ease

Wearing ease is additional inches (centimeters) necessary in a garment, over and above the body measurements. Never use this ease to accommodate a larger size or eliminate it when making pattern adjustments. Refer to the information below for wearing ease for your figure type.

	Misses'	Misses' Petites	Women's
Bust	3" (7.6cm)	3" (7.6cm)	4" (10.2cm)
Waist	1" (25mm)	1" (25mm)	1⅓" (32mm)
Hip	2" (5.1cm)	2" (5.1cm)	4" (10.2cm)

Some patterns may have little or no wearing ease at all. Halter-necks, extremely cut-away armholes, and strapless bodices must fit very closely to the body. If your bust or hips don't match the standard body measurements for your pattern size, you will probably need to adjust the pattern to maintain the original amount of ease.

design ease

The extra fullness added to a garment by the designer, over and above the wearing ease, to create a wide variety of silhouettes is called the design or fashion ease. The different silhouettes are described in the pattern descriptions as close fitting, fitted, semi-fitted, loose fitting and very loose fitting. For dresses, blouses, shirts, tops, vests, jackets and coats, each silhouette describes the fit across the bust. For skirts, culottes and pants, each term describes the fit through the hips.

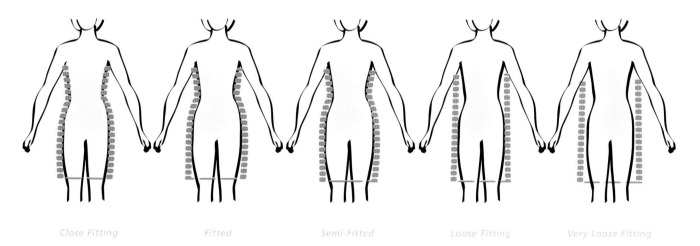

| Close Fitting | Fitted | Semi-Fitted | Loose Fitting | Very Loose Fitting |

patterns and equipment

The pattern envelope presents the total fashion concept originally created by the designer.

envelope front: fashion

It's here you will find the flair of the design as well as the construction details of the garments. Different views may be shown to give you a wider selection of styles. Carefully selected fabrics show the types of fabric, suitable for different seasons that are recommended for this particular pattern. Accessories are chosen to complement the design and to show the fashion concept.

envelope back: information

Use the envelope back to your advantage. All envelope backs contain information you will need to make the proper selection of fabric and notions.

1 Style Number, Size, and Price: Buying information is found on the envelope back.

2 Descriptive Caption: Sizing category, type of garment, and a detailed explanation describing the silhouette, pertinent details not visible in the sketch, and any additional instructions included in the pattern are stated.

3 Body Measurements: Patterns are computed for these measurements. Included in the pattern tissue are wearing ease and design ease as dictated by the design.

4 Notions: All required and optional notions are listed here.

5 Fabrics: Suggestions listed in this area are suitable for the design.
Fabric Design Suitability: This important information tells if the pattern is not suitable for stripes, plaids, or diagonal fabrics. When these fabrics are suitable you'll find a line stating "No Allowance Made for Matching Stripes and Plaids" because the additional yardage (metrage) needed varies with the size of the fabric design.

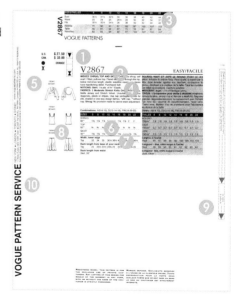

6 Yardage (Metrage): Sizes are across the top. Garment type and/or version letter are just above fabric widths, including interfacing, lining, underlining, and trims needed for each version. Fabric widths have nap indications alongside them.
***/**:** This key indicates whether the yardage (metrage) shown is for fabrics with or without nap. Fabrics with nap (*) have layouts with all pattern pieces placed in the same direction, as required for directional fabrics. Layouts for fabrics without nap (**) may have pattern pieces placed in any direction; additional yardage (metrage) would be required for directional fabrics.

7 Width at Lower Edge: This measurement will tell you the hem circumference of a skirt, dress, shirt, or coat, or the width of the pant leg.

Finished Back Lengths and Side Lengths: These lengths are used as starting points for pattern tissue length adjustments.

8 Back Views: These drawings show styling and construction details for all design versions.

9 Stretch Gauge: Use this measuring method to check the amount of stretch in your fabric. Your fabric must stretch to the end of the Stretch Gauge, to be suitable for a "Knits Only" pattern.

10 Vogue Pattern Service: Vogue Patterns are sold in several countries.

pattern pieces: blueprints

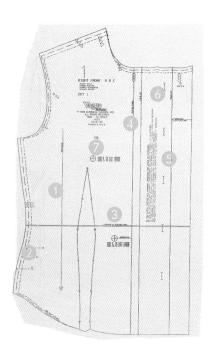

Pattern pieces are the master plans of any sewing project. Each symbol has been printed on your pattern for a very specific purpose. Learn to recognize the markings on each piece and to understand their uses. Then all you have to do is follow them faithfully.

1 Grainline: This heavy solid line with an arrow at one end indicates the direction of the grain. Most often it runs parallel to the fabric selvage, along the lengthwise grain.

2 Cutting Line: Multiple cutting lines are indicated on Multi-Size patterns. The solid outer line is the largest size; broken inner lines are cutting lines for the smaller sizes. A "cut off" line for a style variation may also be found.

3 Adjustment Line: Double lines are printed to indicate areas where lengthening or shortening must be done before cutting, if necessary.

4 Center Front or Center Back Lines: These solid lines indicate where the garment is to fall at the center of the body.

5 Fold Line: This solid line marks where the garment is to be folded during construction.
Roll Line: A solid line shows where the pattern piece is to be softly creased to make a soft, rolling fold.

6 Buttons and Buttonholes: These symbols give you the length of the buttonhole, size of button, and precise location for each.

7 ⊕ This symbol indicates the Bust Point, Waistline, Biceps and Hipline measurements.

Note: All seam allowances are ⅝" (15mm) and included on the pattern piece.

8 Place-on-Fold Bracket: Place piece on the fold of the fabric before cutting.

9 Notches: Used for accurate matching of seams.

10 Symbols ○ ◯ △ ◇ □ **:** These symbols are printed on the tissue pattern for matching seams and construction details.

11 Dart: Corresponding symbols that are to be carefully matched are placed on solid lines that meet at a point to comprise the dart marking.

12 Zipper Placement: This symbol indicates the placement of a zipper on seamline.

13 Hemline: This line states the depth of the hem.

14 Pattern Piece and Version: Name and letter identifies pattern piece. The numbers relate to you the order in which each garment is to be constructed.

Special Cutting Instructions: Any information on the cutting of interfacing, lining, or underlining pertaining to the pattern piece will be found in this enclosed area.

Vogue Pattern Trademark: Your guarantee of fine styling also includes the pattern style number and size.

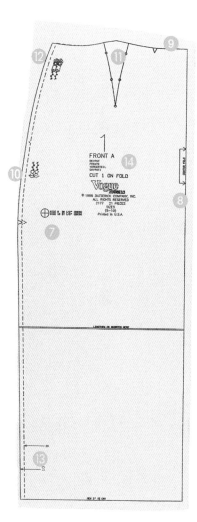

pattern cutting guide

In your Vogue Pattern envelope you will find a Cutting and Sewing Guide along with the actual pattern pieces. This guide can answer almost any question you might have about the general planning, pinning, cutting, and construction of your garment.

The information available in the Cutting Guide is everything in capsule form that you will need to know before you begin to actually sew. Study the correct procedure for preparing your fabric and laying out your pattern.

1 Line Art: This area shows what is contained in the pattern. All style lines and views are shown here.

2 Fabric Cutting Layouts: Helpful hints are given for preparing fabric, arranging fabric for cutting layouts, and for cutting and marking the pattern. Instructions are given for cutting with or without nap, fabrics with pile, shading, or one-way designs. Right and wrong sides are shown for pattern pieces and the fabric.

3 Pattern Pieces: Pattern pieces show fronts and backs, grainlines and piece numbers. Recognition of the actual pattern piece is made simpler by noting this section first. The particular pieces needed for each style are listed.

4 Layout Piece Requirements: All pattern pieces needed for each version of the garment and for underlining, interfacing, and lining are listed.

5 Cutting Guide: The garment cutting layouts are divided into style versions and then into sizes and fabric widths. Each layout is also marked as to suitability for nap. Underlining, interfacing, and lining layouts are also given in the same manner. Pattern pieces to be placed with the printed side up are shown without shading, while those that are to be placed printed side down are shaded. Carefully follow the illustrations when you fold your fabric. If any pattern pieces extend beyond the fold, they are to be cut on a single thickness after all the other pieces are cut. Circle the layout you are using for easy reference.

6 Body Measurements: Complete measurements are given for all sizes for Bust, Waist, Hip and Back Waist Length. Lengths and widths plus additional yardages (metrages) can be included here if there is no room on the envelope back.

Vogue 7063
ENGLISH
Page 1 (3 pages)

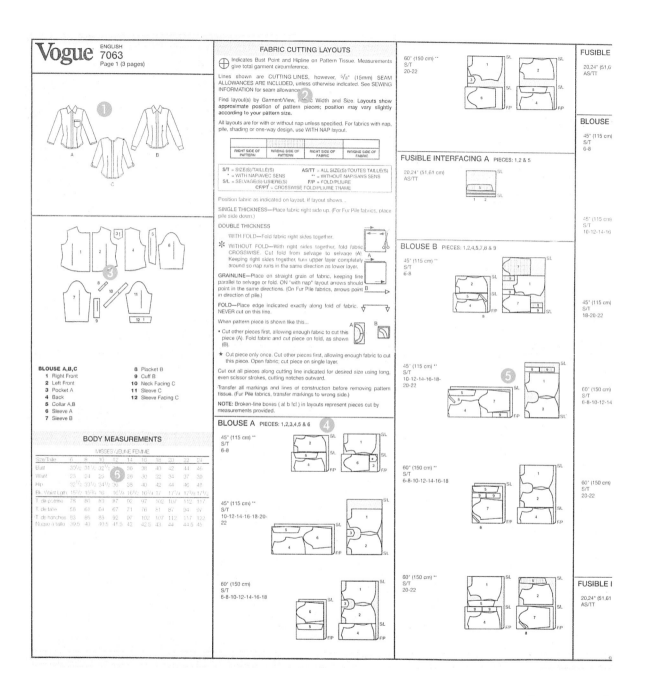

BLOUSE A,B,C
1 Right Front
2 Left Front
3 Pocket A
4 Back
5 Collar A,B
6 Sleeve A
7 Sleeve B

8 Placket B
9 Cuff B
10 Neck Facing C
11 Sleeve C
12 Sleeve Facing C

BODY MEASUREMENTS

MISSES/JEUNE FEMME

Size/Taille	6	8	10	12	14	16	18	20	22	24
Bust	30½	31½	32½	34	36	38	40	42	44	46
Waist	23	24	25	26½	28	30	32	34	37	39
Hip	32½	33½	34½	36	38	40	42	44	46	48
Bk. Waist Lgth.	15½	15¾	16	16¼	16½	16¾	17	17¼	17⅜	17½
T. de poitrine	78	80	83	87	92	97	102	107	112	117
T. de taille	58	61	64	67	71	76	81	87	94	99
T. de hanches	83	85	88	92	97	102	107	112	117	122
Nuque à taille	39.5	40	40.5	41.5	42	42.5	43	44	44.5	45

FABRIC CUTTING LAYOUTS

⊕ Indicates Bust Point and Hipline on Pattern Tissue. Measurements give total garment circumference.

Lines shown are CUTTING LINES, however, ⅝" (15mm) SEAM ALLOWANCES ARE INCLUDED, unless otherwise indicated. See SEWING INFORMATION for seam allowance.

Find layout(s) by Garment/View, Fabric Width and Size. Layouts show approximate position of pattern pieces; position may vary slightly according to your pattern size.

All layouts are for with or without nap unless specified. For fabrics with nap, pile, shading or one-way design, use WITH NAP layout.

RIGHT SIDE OF PATTERN	WRONG SIDE OF PATTERN	RIGHT SIDE OF FABRIC	WRONG SIDE OF FABRIC

S/T = SIZE(S)/TAILLE(S)
* = WITH NAP/AVEC SENS
S/L = SELVAGE(S)/LISIERE(S)
CF/PT = CROSSWISE FOLD/PLIURE TRAME

AS/TT = ALL SIZE(S)/TOUTES TAILLE(S)
** = WITHOUT NAP/SANS SENS
F/P = FOLD/PLIURE

Position fabric as indicated on layout. If layout shows...

SINGLE THICKNESS—Place fabric right side up. (For Fur Pile fabrics, place pile side down.)

DOUBLE THICKNESS

WITH FOLD—Fold fabric right sides together.

✳ WITHOUT FOLD—With right sides together, fold fabric CROSSWISE. Cut fold from selvage to selvage (A). Keeping right sides together, turn upper layer completely around so nap runs in the same direction as lower layer.

GRAINLINE—Place on straight grain of fabric, keeping line parallel to selvage or fold. ON "with nap" layout arrows should point in the same directions. (On Fur Pile fabrics, arrows point in direction of pile.)

FOLD—Place edge indicated exactly along fold of fabric. NEVER cut on this line.

When pattern piece is shown like this...

• Cut other pieces first, allowing enough fabric to cut this piece (A). Fold fabric and cut piece on fold, as shown (B).

★ Cut piece only once. Cut other pieces first, allowing enough fabric to cut this piece. Open fabric; cut piece on single layer.

Cut out all pieces along cutting line indicated for desired size using long, even scissor strokes, cutting notches outward.

Transfer all markings and lines of construction before removing pattern tissue. (Fur Pile fabrics, transfer markings to wrong side.)

NOTE: Broken-line boxes (a! b !c!) in layouts represent pieces cut by measurements provided.

BLOUSE A PIECES: 1,2,3,4,5 & 6

45" (115 cm) **
S/T
6-8

45" (115 cm) **
S/T
10-12-14-16-18-20-22

60" (150 cm)
S/T
6-8-10-12-14-16-18

60" (150 cm) **
S/T
20-22

FUSIBLE INTERFACING A PIECES: 1,2 & 5

20,24" (51,61 cm)
AS/TT

BLOUSE B PIECES: 1,2,4,5,7,8 & 9

45" (115 cm) **
S/T
6-8

45" (115 cm) **
S/T
10-12-14-16-18-20-22

60" (150 cm) **
S/T
6-8-10-12-14-16-18

60" (150 cm) **
S/T
20-22

FUSIBLE

20,24" (51,61
AS/TT

BLOUSE

45" (115 cm)
S/T
6-8

45" (115 cm)
S/T
10-12-14-16

45" (115 cm)
S/T
18-20-22

60" (150 cm)
S/T
6-8-10-12-14

60" (150 cm)
S/T
20-22

FUSIBLE I

20,24" (51,61
AS/TT

pattern sewing guide

On the reverse side of the Cutting Guide you will find a step-by-step Sewing Guide arranged by garment versions with organized instructions for fast reading and comprehension. At the top of the sheet is the illustration key and suggestions on stitching, trimming, and pressing, which can serve as excellent reminders.

A glossary of sewing terms has definitions of each term to help you understand each sewing technique used in the construction.

The Cutting and Sewing Guides are indispensable ingredients; following the instructions diligently can help to make the most professional looking garment possible.

1 Pattern Identification: The pattern number is given along with the page number. Pages are numbered consecutively, stating the amount you will find.

2 Fabric Illustration Key: This explains the use of shading and texture in technical sketches. We follow the same distinctions throughout the illustrations in this book.

3 Helpful Hints: Important points to remember on stitching, trimming, and pressing are shown and explained for your benefit.

4 Titles: The construction procedures for different parts of the garment and the individual versions are presented separately.

5 Sewing Directions: Construction of each garment section is explained individually and every procedure is shown consecutively for quick reference.

6 Construction Sketches: Many sewing techniques are easier to understand when they are illustrated. Use them with the written instructions.

7 Enlarged View: You will find that details of important and/or difficult construction areas are enlarged and circled to clarify the sewing procedure involved.

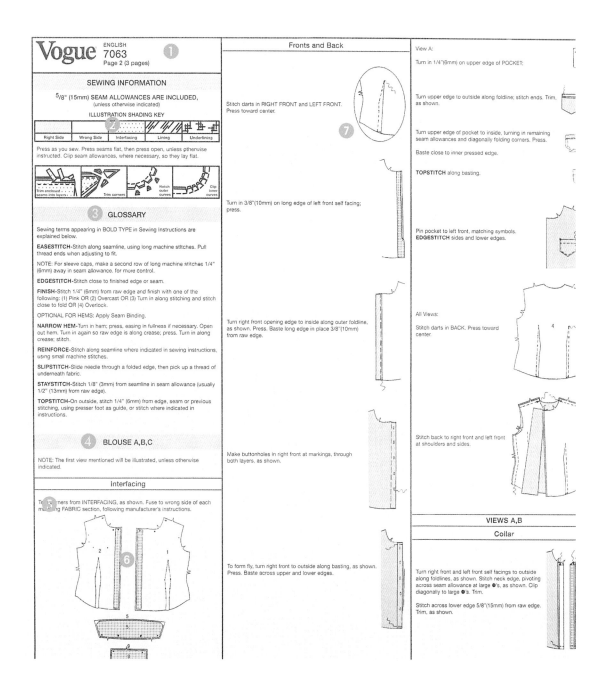

SEWING INFORMATION

5/8" (15mm) SEAM ALLOWANCES ARE INCLUDED,
(unless otherwise indicated)

ILLUSTRATION SHADING KEY

Right Side	Wrong Side	Interfacing	Lining	Underlining

Press as you sew. Press seams flat, then press open, unless otherwise instructed. Clip seam allowances, where necessary, so they lay flat.

Trim enclosed seams into layers.   Trim corners   Notch outer curves   Clip inner curves

GLOSSARY

Sewing terms appearing in BOLD TYPE in Sewing Instructions are explained below.

EASESTITCH-Stitch along seamline, using long machine stitches. Pull thread ends when adjusting to fit.

NOTE: For sleeve caps, make a second row of long machine stitches 1/4" (6mm) away in seam allowance, for more control.

EDGESTITCH-Stitch close to finished edge or seam.

FINISH-Stitch 1/4" (6mm) from raw edge and finish with one of the following: (1) Pink OR (2) Overcast OR (3) Turn in along stitching and stitch close to fold OR (4) Overlock.

OPTIONAL FOR HEMS: Apply Seam Binding.

NARROW HEM-Turn in hem; press, easing in fullness if necessary. Open out hem. Turn in again so raw edge is along crease; press. Turn in along crease; stitch.

REINFORCE-Stitch along seamline where indicated in sewing instructions, using small machine stitches.

SLIPSTITCH-Slide needle through a folded edge, then pick up a thread of underneath fabric.

STAYSTITCH-Stitch 1/8" (3mm) from seamline in seam allowance (usually 1/2" (13mm) from raw edge).

TOPSTITCH-On outside, stitch 1/4" (6mm) from edge, seam or previous stitching, using presser foot as guide, or stitch where indicated in instructions.

BLOUSE A,B,C

NOTE: The first view mentioned will be illustrated, unless otherwise indicated.

Interfacing

Trim corners from INTERFACING, as shown. Fuse to wrong side of each matching FABRIC section, following manufacturer's instructions.

Fronts and Back

Stitch darts in RIGHT FRONT and LEFT FRONT. Press toward center.

Turn in 3/8"(10mm) on long edge of left front self facing; press.

Turn right front opening edge to inside along outer foldline, as shown. Press. Baste long edge in place 3/8"(10mm) from raw edge.

Make buttonholes in right front at markings, through both layers, as shown.

To form fly, turn right front to outside along basting, as shown. Press. Baste across upper and lower edges.

View A:

Turn in 1/4"(6mm) on upper edge of POCKET;

Turn upper edge to outside along foldline; stitch ends. Trim, as shown.

Turn upper edge of pocket to inside, turning in remaining seam allowances and diagonally folding corners. Press.

Baste close to inner pressed edge.

TOPSTITCH along basting.

Pin pocket to left front, matching symbols. **EDGESTITCH** sides and lower edges.

All Views:

Stitch darts in BACK. Press toward center.

Stitch back to right front and left front at shoulders and sides.

VIEWS A,B

Collar

Turn right front and left front self facings to outside along foldlines, as shown. Stitch neck edge, pivoting across seam allowance at large ●'s, as shown. Clip diagonally to large ●'s. Trim.

Stitch across lower edge 5/8"(15mm) from raw edge. Trim, as shown.

notions: your sewing accessories

It is a good idea to keep on hand a supply of the more standard notions, like pins, needles, snaps, and hooks and eyes, so you don't have to continually interrupt your sewing to purchase some small item you have forgotten. Some notions you will have to buy each time you purchase fabric to ensure that they will match and be appropriate to your particular fabric and style; buttons, thread, zippers, and bindings or tapes are perfect examples. Since the notions counter contains a seemingly endless array of gadgets, use the back of your pattern envelope and the following descriptions to guide your selection.

pins

Pins vary in size and type. Pin size is stated in sixteenths of an inch according to length: a size 16 is $^{16}/_{16}$" or 1" (25mm) long; a size 8 is ½" (13mm) long. For general sewing, #17 (1$^{1}/_{16}$" or 26mm) dressmaker pins are most commonly used. These are slender pins of medium diameter. Ballpoint pins should be used on knitted fabrics as their rounded tips slip between the yarns to avoid snags.

All pins must be rustproof brass, nickel-plated steel or stainless steel. Plastic or glass headed pins are available in various sizes and are easy to see on the fabric. Glass headed pins are extremely heat resistant.

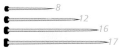

hand sewing needles

The shape of the eye, the length and the point, each designed for a specific use, classifies hand-sewing needles. Choose the type of needle according to the job it will be doing, and the size of needle according to the thread it will be pulling through the fabric. The finer or sheerer the fabric, the sharper and more slender the needle should be.

Two size scales are generally used for needles—1 through 10, and 14 through 22. For each needle type, the smaller the size number, the longer and thicker the needle. Sizes 7 through 10 are best for most dressmaking, while the other sizes are for heavier or specialized sewing.

DRESSMAKING NEEDLES

SHARPS are all-purpose medium-length needles with small, rounded eyes used for general sewing.

BETWEENS are shorter needles with small, rounded eyes used for detailed handwork and quilting requiring short, fine stitches.

sharps
betweens
milliner's
embroidery

MILLINER'S needles are long with small, rounded eyes used for long basting stitches, gathering, and millinery work.

EMBROIDERY needles are medium-length with long oval eyes; generally used for embroidery and crewelwork, they can also be substituted for sharps.

Needles are also available with ballpoint tips for use with knitted fabrics. The slightly rounded tip slips between the yarns to help prevent snagging the fabric. Easy threading, self-threading or calyx eye needles have a slot on the outer eye for easy threading.

polyester thread

cotton-covered polyester thread

mercerized cotton thread

thread

A quality thread is strong, smooth, and consistent in thickness, and it resists tangling. Select the proper thread according to fabric weight, purpose, and color. Thread should be the same color or slightly darker than the fabric. For multicolored prints and plaids, select thread colors according to the predominant hue in the fabric.

POLYESTER THREAD, either 100% polyester or cotton covered, provides strength and elasticity for sewing on fabrics made of synthetic, natural, or blended fibers. It is especially desirable for knit, stretch, and permanent-press fabrics because of its stretch and recovery, and its non-shrinkage. 100% polyester thread can be made from strands of long staple polyester multifilament or spun short staple multifilament, which are then twisted tightly together.

Twisting together two or more strands of polyester multifilament wrapped with mercerized cotton forms cotton-covered polyester cord thread. The cotton sheath provides resistance to heat, while the polyester cord gives strength and elasticity. Polyester thread is available in different weights for specific uses: extra fine for lightweight fabrics; all-purpose for general sewing; topstitching and buttonhole twist for decorative stitching and hand-worked buttonholes; button and carpet thread for hand sewing buttons and extra strength; and machine and hand quilting thread.

MERCERIZED COTTON THREAD is strong and lustrous, without any stretch or give, for use on woven natural fiber fabrics. It is formed by twisting together two or three strands of spun staple cotton fibers that have been mercerized for added strength, luster, affinity for dye, and color fastness. Size 50, a medium diameter thread, is suitable for hand and machine sewing on light and medium weight fabrics. Size 40, a heavier thread, is used for heavier fabrics, slipcovers, and draperies as well as machine embroidery.

buttons

Make your buttons work as an accent to your garment. Although buttons are available in a wide range of shapes and contours, there are basically only two types. A sew-through button has two to four holes for attaching the button to the garment. A shank button has a metal, plastic, or fabric shank behind the button through which the button is attached. The shank allows room for the overlapping fabric so that the button rests on top of the buttonhole.

To determine button size, use this button gauge.

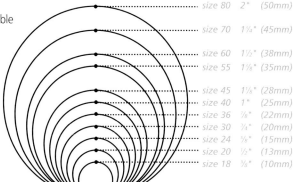

size 80   2"   (50mm)
size 70   1¼"   (45mm)
size 60   1½"   (38mm)
size 55   1⅛"   (35mm)
size 45   1⅛"   (28mm)
size 40   1"   (25mm)
size 36   ⅞"   (22mm)
size 30   ¾"   (20mm)
size 24   ⅝"   (15mm)
size 20   ½"   (13mm)
size 18   ⅛"   (10mm)

zippers

Zippers are available in a variety of colors, sizes, and weights for almost any conceivable fastening task. Choose a zipper according to the style needed for your garment opening and a weight that is compatible with your fabric. The conventional zipper, the most common type, can be used for most standard zipper applications on most garments. Specialty zippers designed for specific openings or garments are also available.

The weight of a zipper is determined by its construction and the type of tape used. A coil-constructed zipper is made from a continuous strand of nylon or polyester twisted into a spiral and attached to a woven or knitted synthetic tape. It is lightweight and flexible, yet very strong, and is ideal for light and medium weight fabrics and all types of knits.

A chain-constructed zipper has metal or plastic teeth attached to a cotton or cotton-blend tape. It is a little heavier and more rigid than the coils; some metal styles are excellent for heavy-duty use.

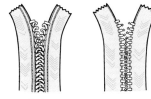

coil zipper   chain zipper

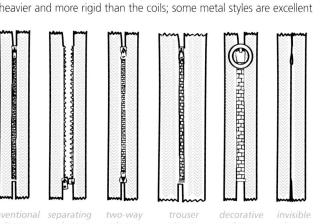

conventional   separating   two-way   trouser   decorative   invisible
zipper   zipper   zipper   zipper   zipper   zipper

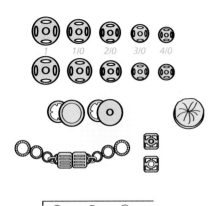

fasteners

SNAPS, used for closing and anchoring garments, are available in many sizes and types. Snaps come in nickel or black enamel-coated metal with the smaller sizes, 4/0 to 1 (6mm to 11mm), being the most popular. The larger sizes, 2 to 4 (13mm to 17mm), are suitable for heavy-duty use. Large silk-covered snaps, ideal for suits and coats, are available in neutral colors. You may cover your own for special color combinations or purchase see-through nylon snaps to blend with the color of your garment. For casual clothes and children's wear, snaps on cotton tape and no-sew snap fasteners applied with special pliers or attaching tool can be used. Fur snaps are perfect for attaching fur collars and other accessories to your garment.

HOOKS AND EYES come in a variety of designs for special holding purposes. The standard type is made with brass, nickel, or black enamel finish, and comes in sizes 00 to 2 for lightweight fabrics and sizes 3 to 5 for bulky and heavyweight fabrics. The eye can be curved or straight.

Large hooks and eyes, either plain or covered, make sturdy fastenings for coats or other items, especially fur. Specially shaped hook and bar closures, both sew-on and prong, make practical fasteners for waistbands on skirts and pants. Hooks and eyes are also available on cotton tape.

HOOK AND LOOP TAPE consists of two strips, one with tiny hooks and one with a looped pile, that intermesh when pressed together and open when peeled apart. It is also sold in precut shapes and by the yard.

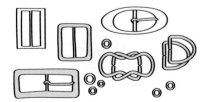

BUCKLES are available in a wide variety of shapes and sizes, with or without prongs. They come in all types of materials such as metal, wood, plastic, and leather; or they may be covered with fabric for a custom finish. They can be purchased singly or in kits with belting. Eyelets are available with a nickel, gilt, or colored enamel finish and are applied with special pliers or attaching tool. They can be used for belts, lacing, and decorative ties.

elastic

Elastics are available in many different types and widths to be used in casings or applied directly to the garment. Elastics are made from a rubber or stretchable synthetic core that is wrapped with cotton, synthetic fiber, or a blend of fibers. Elastic thread is a very thin, covered core that is used for shirring. Elastic cord is a round or oval covered cord in varying diameters that can be sewn directly to the garment or used for loop closings.

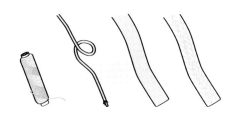

tapes and trims

Tapes, laces, and bindings in matching colors will give the inside of your garment a custom-made look—not to mention perfectly finished edges!

SEAM BINDING is used for finishing hem edges and straight facing edges. Ribbon seam binding is a woven tape approximately ½" (13mm) wide, which can be used to reinforce or extend seams. Lace seam binding provides a decorative finish on seams and hems; stretch lace is suitable for use on knitted fabrics. Available prepackaged in a wide range of colors.

BIAS TAPE is available in a variety of widths with pre-folded edges to use for binding curved or straight edges, casings, ties, and trims. Single-fold bias tape is ½" (13mm) wide with edges folded to the wrong side and meeting at the center. Double-fold is ¼" (6mm) wide and has been folded again just slightly off-center; it is also available in an extra wide ½" (13mm) width. Wide bias tape is ⅞" to 1" (22mm to 25mm) wide with edges folded ¼" (6mm) to the wrong side. Stretchable lace binding is also available. Prepackaged in a wide range of colors and prints.

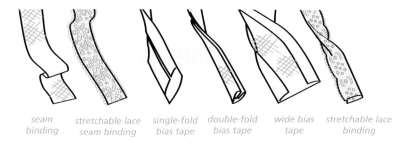

seam binding   stretchable lace seam binding   single-fold bias tape   double-fold bias tape   wide bias tape   stretchable lace binding

HEM FACING is a 2" (50mm) wide bias tape or lace strip used for facing hems and binding edges. Prepackaged in many colors.

hem facing   stretchable lace hem facing

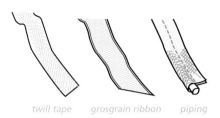

twill tape grosgrain ribbon piping

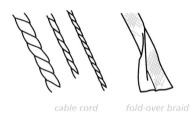

cable cord fold-over braid

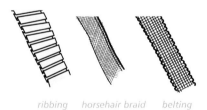

ribbing horsehair braid belting

more tapes and trims

TWILL TAPE is firmly woven tape used in tailoring and for reinforcing seams. It comes in black, natural and white in ¼", ½", ¾", and 1" (6mm, 13mm, 20mm and 25mm) widths.

GROSGRAIN RIBBON is firmly woven, ribbed ribbon used for staying waistlines, facing waistbands and belts, and for decorative trims. It is available in a wide range of widths, colors and patterns.

PIPING is a narrow, corded, bias strip with a ¼" (6mm) seam allowance, which is inserted into a seam for a decorative accent. It comes in several colors in prepackaged lengths.

CABLE CORD can be used as filler for piping, cording, tubing, and trapunto and for making corded buttonholes and tucks. It is sold by the yard (meter) in various diameters.

FOLD-OVER BRAID is a knitted braid with finished edges that is folded in half, usually with one edge slightly wider than the other. Used for binding and trimming raw edges. It's available in different colors and designs, prepackaged and by the yard (meter).

RIBBING is a knitted band with a variety of types, weights, and widths used to finish necklines, armholes or a waistline of a garment. The stretchability varies, depending upon the knit—some are quite stable while others are very stretchy. It's available prepackaged or by the yard (meter).

HORSEHAIR BRAID is stiff, bias braid woven of transparent synthetic yarns. It's used to stiffen hem edges, especially on evening and bridal wear. Available in different widths.

BELTING is a very stiff band used to reinforce self-covered belts and waistbands, and available in both regular and iron-on types. Sold in prepackaged lengths or by the yard (meter) in ½" to 3" (13mm to 75mm) widths.

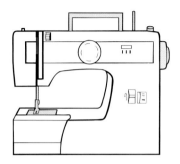

Sewing machines have become very sophisticated today with the advancement of the computer age. With the introduction of new fabrics, new needles and presser feet have been designed to meet the demands of the fashion sewer. When buying a new machine, it is important for you to analyze what type of sewing you currently do and what you would like to do in the future. Follow your sewing machine manual for operating instructions.

All sewing machines share one important feature, no matter the number of stitches they offer—**the thread tension**. The strength of your seams depends on the correct thread tension. Before stitching on any garment, you should test the tension on a scrap of fabric on both the lengthwise and crosswise grains. Before adjusting your tension, check your thread choice and needle size for the fabric you sewing on. For normal sewing, you should be stitching with the same type thread through your needle and on your bobbin. A too large or too small needle will affect your stitch quality also.

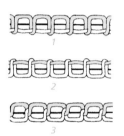

As a general rule, your should only adjust your upper tension. In most cases, the bobbin tension has been factory set. The upper tension controls the thread that passes through the needle. If it is **too loose**, the needle thread will pull through to the underside of your fabric (1). If the bobbin thread shows through on the top and the needle thread lies flat on the surface; your upper tension is **too tight** (2). For a **balanced tension**, both threads are drawn equally into the fabric (3).

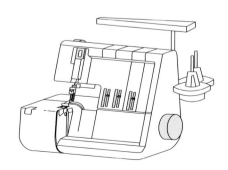

The overlock machine, or serger, has become almost commonplace in everyone's sewing room today. The serger trims the fabric while overcasting the edges at the same time.

Numerous models with a variety of stitch formations are now available from most sewing machine manufacturers. The serger can be used to sew seams just as easily as it can finish fabric edges or apply decorative trims.

Choose your serger with the type of sewing you are doing now and what you want to do in the future. Follow the serger manual for complete operating instructions.

basic sewing tools

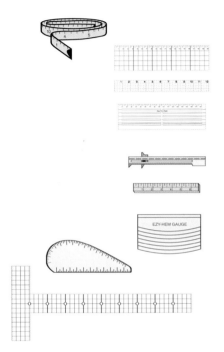

measuring tools

Measuring tools are among the most important items in your sewing box. The key to success is to measure often and accurately.

Tape measures should be 60" (152cm) long with metal tips and made of a material that will not stretch. It is most helpful if the numbers, in inches or centimeters, are printed on both sides.

Rulers are necessary for all your sewing projects. You should have at least one 12–18" (30.5–46cm) long, and one 5–6" (12.5–15cm) long. They can be found in a variety of materials and should have a metal edge for accuracy. The plastic see-through type is well suited for buttonholes, pleats, etc. and can readily serve all your needs. The numbers should be clearly indicated.

Yardsticks are invaluable for general marking purposes. Those made of metal are sturdiest.

A **sewing gauge** is a 6" (15cm) metal or plastic ruler with a sliding indicator. It is ideal for quick, accurate measurements of hems, buttonholes and pleats.

A **hem gauge** is generally made of lightweight metal with one gradually curved edge designed to accommodate the shape of your hems. The different hem depths are clearly indicated on it surface.

A **French curve** is used to redraw curved areas such as armholes, necklines, and princess seams when altering patterns.

T-squares can be made of either clear plastic or metal. Use it for straightening grain, locating opposite grains, altering your pattern tissue, or for other marking tasks.

A **skirt marker** is the quickest, easiest and most accurate way to mark hems. There are several types: pin, chalk and a combination of both.

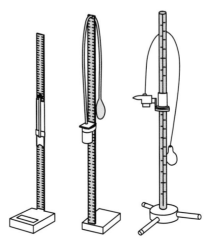

cutting tools

It is vital to be accurate when cutting out the individual pieces of your garment. With that in mind, your cutting tools become some of the most important pieces of sewing equipment you will own.

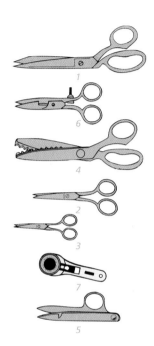

Dressmaker's shears are bent-handle shears with 7" or 8" (18 or 21cm) blades hinged with a screw. The bent handles are preferred because the fabric can rest flat on the table when being cut. (1)

Sewing scissors have small round handles and are used for more delicate cutting and trimming. (2)

Embroidery scissors are used for buttonholes and detail work. (3)

Pinking shears are used to finish raw edges of fabrics that do not ravel easily. (4)

Thread clips are a scissor variation with short blades and an inner spring mechanism to keep them apart. (5)

Buttonhole scissors are constructed to allow you to begin cutting within the body of the fabric. A screw and nut arrangement makes it possible to set the blades to cut only a pre-scribed length. (6)

Rotary cutters are similar to a pizza cutter and are used with a special self-healing mat and plastic ruler for accurate cutting. Replaceable blades are available. (7)

marking tools

Marking plays an important role in the construction process. The pattern tissue has specific construction lines and symbols printed on its surface for you to transfer to your garment pieces. If you have been accurate in marking these guidelines, construction will be greatly simplified and errors kept to a minimum.

Since you will be working with many varieties of fabric, you should have on hand the different types of marking equipment.

Chalk is ideal for marking most fabrics. Easy to use it comes in many forms such as clay chalk wedges or squares, chalk wheels, chalk marking pencils, and wax chalk. (1). A soapstone marker is an alternative to chalk pencils and can easily be removed. (2)

Fabric marking pens work well on most washable fabrics. There are different types of pens, air-, water- and heat soluble. Air-soluble disappears in the air within 12 to 48 hours. Water-soluble rinse away with water. Some markings will disappear when ironed. (3)

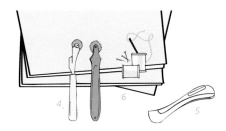

Tracing wheels and ***dressmaker's tracing paper*** is suitable for most fine fabrics. (4).

A **hera** marking tool is a Japanese tool that marks the fabric when pressure is applied leaving an indentation. It works best on natural fiber fabrics (5).

Thread tracing is used to mark pockets, garment centerlines, tailor tacks, grainlines or for general basting. Choose thread in a slightly contrasting color for easier removal (6).

sewing aids

These additional sewing aids help contribute to fine workmanship. They enable you to perform your hand tasks more quickly and easily.

A **seam ripper** is a simple and safe pen-like device that allows careful ripping of adjustments and mistakes. (1)

Pins and **Pincushions** are essential tools in any sewing room either used on the tabletop or on your wrist. At least one should be filled with fine emery for sharpening and removing rust from your needles and pins. (2)

Sewing tape is measured on one side to use as a stitching guide, especially when topstitching. One type can be separated into various widths. (3)

Basting tape is very narrow and has adhesive on both sides. Use it to hold a zipper in place or two layers of fabric for stitching. Do not stitch over tape and be sure to remove it after sewing the seam. (4)

Liquid seam sealant prevents fabrics from fraying. Use it to secure thread ends on buttonholes, serger seams, prevent fraying on seam allowances, or ends of ribbons. (5)

A **magnetic seam guide** attaches to the bed of the sewing machine next to the needle plate. Adjust it easily to ensure uniform stitching and seam allowances. (6)

A **needle threader** is a small device to help you on those frustrating days when you just can't thread your needle. (7)

Iron cleaner is used to remove any residue left on the bottom of your iron after working with fusibles. (8)

pressing tools

The real secret of success in sewing is to press as you sew. Careful, thorough treatment during each stage of construction will result in a good-looking garment that requires only a light touch-up when completed. You will find that it is quicker and easier to press in units as you sew. For example, stitch and press all darts and pocket flaps, and so on.

The *iron* should combine the characteristics of both a steam iron and a dry iron. The steam vents should be located at the end of the soleplate to provide concentrated steam when it is needed. Be sure the iron has a wide temperature range for the best care of all you fashion fabrics. A controlled spray and surge of steam mechanism can also be helpful. (1)

An *iron cover* is placed over the soleplate of your iron and is used instead of a press cloth to prevent shine and scorching. (2)

The *ironing board* should be sturdy, level and adjustable to different heights. Pad the board with cotton batting or purchased padding already cut to fit. Place a silicone-treated cover over the surface to prevent scorching or sticking. Keep the cover smooth and clean.

Press cloths should be selected in relation to the weight of your fabric.They should be similar in weight for best results. Have at least three on hand: a transparent variety for seeing details, a two-part wool and cotton type for most general pressing needs, and a non-stick or Teflon™ type for fusibles. (3).

A *tailor's ham* is an oblong, firmly stuffed cushion with subtly rounded curves. It is designed for pressing the curved areas of your garment such as darts, sleeve caps, princess seams, or any place that requires a rounded, curved shape pressed in. (4).

A *press mitt* is similar to a tailor's ham, but small enough to fit over your hand. (5).

A *seam roll* is a long, firmly stuffed, tubular cushion that is rounded at each end. It is used to press small, curved areas and long seams in hard-to-reach areas such as sleeves. (6).

A *sleeve board* is actually two small ironing boards attached one on top of the other. They are designed for pressing small or slim areas, such as sleeves or necklines that do not fit over your regular board. (7).

Of course, there are many more sewing tools and equipment available than listed here. Feel free to add to your collection whenever necessary.

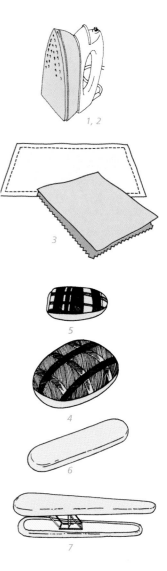

prepare to sew

Before preparing and cutting your fabric, it is important to understand the terminology for woven and knitted fabrics. Here is some common terminology used when talking about fabrics that will help you sound like a pro.

Grain—the direction in which the threads composing the fabric run. Every woven fabric consists of crosswise threads worked under and over the more sturdy lengthwise threads.

Selvage—the narrow, flat, woven border resulting at both lengthwise sides when the crosswise threads change direction. The threads composing it are strong and densely woven. This border is a pre-finished edge, and may be used to advantage for center back seams, waistbands, as a stay instead of twill tape, and much more.

Lengthwise Grain—the direction of the lengthwise threads running parallel to the selvage. These threads are very strong and stable, as they must withstand great tension during the weaving process. Generally, fabrics are cut along the lengthwise grain for this reason. Sometimes know as "straight-of-fabric" or "straight-of-goods".

Crosswise Grain—the direction of the crosswise threads, running from selvage to selvage at right angles to the lengthwise threads. In most fabrics, it has a very slight amount of give.

Bias—any diagonal intersecting the lengthwise and crosswise threads. Fabric cut on the bias possesses much greater elasticity than that cut on the crosswise grain.

True Bias—is obtained by folding the on-grain fabric diagonally so the crosswise threads are parallel to the selvage. True bias exists at any 45° angle to any straight edge of fabric whose lengthwise and crosswise threads are perpendicular.

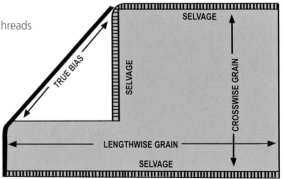

preparing your fabric

Carefully steam-press your fabric to remove any wrinkles or foldlines. In some fabrics, such as knits and permanent-finish fabrics, the crease may not always be removed by pressing. For these fabrics, avoid layouts where the pattern pieces are placed on the fold. You may need to figure a new layout that avoids the crease altogether or places the crease in an inconspicuous place.

straightening fabric

Woven Fabrics—Straighten ends to coincide with the crosswise threads by snipping close to the selvage and pulling a crosswise thread, this will cause the fabric to pucker… keep pulling the thread along the entire edge and then cut along the puckered line. This is the most time consuming method, but it is the most accurate. If the crosswise thread is readily visible, then just cut directly.

Another method is to snip and then tear the fabric, use extreme caution with this method; the pulling action may throw the first several inches off grain at both fabric ends.

Knitted Fabrics—straighten the fabric ends by cutting along a crosswise line of loops. If loops are not easily seen, it may be necessary to first mark the line of loops with a marker or even thread tracing. These markings can be used for determining if the knit is on-grain or not. A tubular knit can be cut open lengthwise following a rib or lengthwise row of loops.

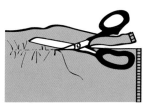

woven fabric

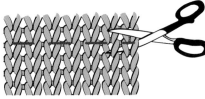

knitted fabric

straightening grain

It is vital to the final appearance of your garment to find the straight grain of the fabric. Your fabric is on grain when crosswise and lengthwise threads or loops are at perfect right angles to each other.

➤ Check the grain after ends of your fabric have been evened out.

➤ If the edges do not align along all three sides, then the fabric is off grain and must be straightened.

➤ If edges are even; check to see if the corners form a right angle by aligning a corner of your fabric with your cutting surface.

➤ For knitted fabrics, match only the ends; the lengthwise edges of a knit may not always be straight.

If the fabric is only slightly off grain, it can be straightened by steam-pressing the threads into proper alignment. To do this, fold the fabric right sides together, and then pin together every 5"(13cm) along the selvages and ends. You may need to pin the fabric to the ironing board to keep it square. Press firmly, stroking from the selvages toward the fold.

If your fabric is very off-grain, it can be straightened by pulling the fabric gently but firmly in the opposite direction from the way the ends slant until a perfect right angle corner is formed. If fabric is washable, place it in warm water for a few minutes to help relax the finish before pulling the fabric ends. Then pin a selvage to a taut clothesline every few inches or lay on a flat surface and allow to dry. Repeat if necessary.

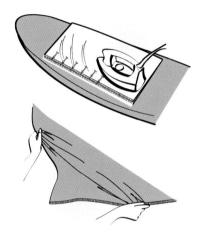

Note that permanent finish fabrics cannot be straightened. It is perfectly all right to use them as they are, matching and pinning the selvage only, not the ends.

Some printed fabrics may not be off grain but the print design does not coincide with the grainline. These fabrics should be avoided. If you must use them, you must allow the print design to dictate the layout, not the grain.

preshrinking

Many fabrics on today's market may not require preshrinking. Always read the label on the fabric bolt to determine the specifics on shrinkage and the suggested care for the fabric. If you are unsure, it is always safer to preshrink your fabric rather than discover a shrinkage problem after your garment is completed.

Washing or dry cleaning can also help to remove resins used for finishing some knitted or woven fabrics that could cause skipped stitches.

For washable fabrics, you can launder and dry the fabric following the same methods you will use on the finished garment.

Another method is to fold the fabric evenly and immerse in hot water for thirty minutes to one hour. Gently squeeze out the water and dry according to the fabric care instructions.

Dry cleanable fabrics should be shrunk by a professional dry cleaner, if possible.

cut with care

By now your fabric is fully prepared and any pattern alterations needed should also be done. Circle the correct layout for your version, size, and appropriate fabric width on your Cutting Guide. Be sure to use the "with nap" layout if your fabric is a knit or has a nap or pile, shading, or a one-way design. The pattern layout provides you with a completely reliable guide for laying out your pattern swiftly and economically. You can't bend the rules by laying some pieces a little off grain to fit. A simple maneuver like this can jeopardize all your future efforts on that garment—one side of the skirt may flare more than the other, the entire bodice section might ripple and pull, and facings cut off-grain will pucker.

layouts

Here are some ideas used by professionals—suggestions to follow as you lay out and cut your pattern for perfect results every time.

- Pin fabric every three inches (7.5cm) or so on indicated foldline and along all ends and selvages. The selvages may have to be clipped every few inches (centimeters) so that the fabric will lie flat. For knitted fabrics, match straightened ends or thread trace along one rib near center of fabric to use as lengthwise foldline or for aligning crosswise fold.
- Extend a short grainline to pattern ends with pencil, and measure often to be sure that the pattern is placed on the correct grain.
- Double-check all alterations to see that seam and cutting lines are redrawn and all corresponding pieces are altered, including facings.
- Lay out all pattern pieces before you begin cutting to be sure you have enough fabric.
- Place pattern pieces printed side up unless otherwise indicated by the Cutting Guide. All layouts are for with or without nap unless specified.

RIGHT SIDE OF PATTERN	WRONG SIDE OF PATTERN	RIGHT SIDE OF FABRIC	WRONG SIDE OF FABRIC

S/T = SIZE(S)/TAILLE(S)	**AS/TT** = ALL SIZE(S)/TOUTES TAILLE(S)
* = WITH NAP/AVEC SENS	** = WITHOUT NAP/SANS SENS
S/L = SELVAGE(S)/LISIERE(S)	**F/P** = FOLD/PLIURE
CF/PT = CROSSWISE FOLD/PLIURE TRAME	

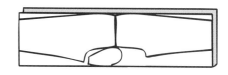

With Fold—fabric is folded in half on the lengthwise grain, right sides together, matching selvages.

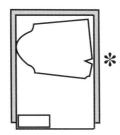
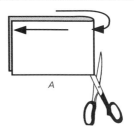
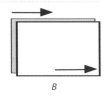

Without Fold—fabric is folded in half with right sides together on the crosswise grain of the fabric, matching selvages. Cut from selvage to selvage. (A) Turn the upper layer completely around so nap runs in same direction as lower layer. (B) This layout will be marked with a large asterisk.

A

B

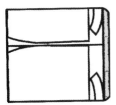

Double Fold—fabric is folded twice along the lengthwise grain, right sides together, with the selvages usually meeting in the center.

Single Layer—fabric is opened up to single thickness and placed right side up. For fur pile fabrics, place pile side down.

Partial Fold—fabric is folded with right sides together on lengthwise grain, only wide enough to fit the width of the pattern piece or pieces on the fold. Other pattern pieces are placed on the single layer of fabric above the folded portion.

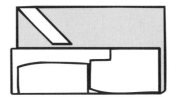

Stars are used to indicate that the pattern piece is cut only once on a single layer of fabric. When your layout shows a pattern piece with a star, extending beyond the fabric fold, cut the other pieces first, then unfold the fabric, and cut out the remaining pattern piece.

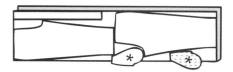

If the fabric design must be matched, always take care to match seamlines, not cutting lines.

cutting

- Pin first along lengthwise grainlines and foldlines.
- Place pins perpendicular to and ¼" (6mm) inside the cutting line and diagonally at the corners of the pattern, spacing them about every three or four inches (7.5cm or 10cm) apart, or closer for sheer or slippery fabrics.
- Use long, bent-handled shears, and cut with steady, even slashes. Never cut out a pattern with pinking shears. Use them only to finish seams during construction.
- To avoid distorting the fabric, cut "directionally" with the grain. Never lift the fabric from the table. Keep one hand flat on the pattern piece while cutting.
- Use the point of the scissors to cut notches outward. Cut groups of notches in continuous blocks for easier matching.
- Be sure to use each pattern piece the correct number of times. Such details as pockets, cuffs, welts, and belt carriers are likely to need more than the usual two pieces.
- Fold the cut pieces softly and lay them on a flat surface.
- Save fabric scraps left from cutting. They are often needed for such things as bound buttonholes, sleeve plackets, and other sections not cut from pattern pieces; or for testing tension, stitch length, and pressing techniques.

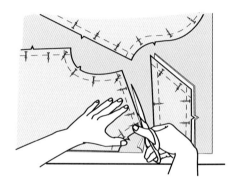

directional fabrics

If you have been avoiding fabrics that require special layouts, such as napped or pile fabrics, diagonals, plaids, stripes, and border prints, let us dispel your fears. You can usually use the same methods for preparing, pinning, and cutting, but do give more than average attention to laying out your pattern pieces and basting the garment together.

Fabrics with nap, pile, shading, or one-way designs must be cut with all pattern pieces placed in the same direction. If your pattern suggests these fabrics, your Fabric Cutting Layout includes a "with nap" layout, which you must follow.

matching your fabric design at seams

Use the following tips to match your motif, plaid or diagonal fabric design at seamlines.

- The pattern pieces should be placed so the notches and the symbols along the seamlines are matched at the center and sides.
- Center seams must be placed with the seamline directly in the center of a motif or plaid repeat for a straight seam.
- A shaped seam (center or side) should start out in the center of a motif repeat, if possible, so when the seams are joined, the design will chevron. The angle will depend on the shape of the seam.
- Always match the seamlines, not the cutting lines.
- Try to match motifs at the front armhole seamline at the notch. The curve of the sleeve cap may make it impossible to match the plaid around the rest of the armhole.
- Diagonals are difficult to match—darts, shoulder seams, etc.
- Side seams will not match above the dart.
- Lapel facings should be cut from the same part of the motif as the bodice.

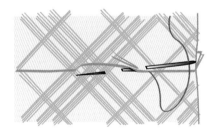

Slip Basting: Slip basting will help to ensure a perfectly matched motif. To slip baste, work from the right side of the fabric. Crease and turn under the seam allowance along one edge, lay the folded edge in position on the corresponding piece, matching the plaid at the seamline, and pin. Slip the needle through the upper fold, then through the lower layer using a single long stitch. Continue this stitch for the entire length of the seam. You can now machine stitch the seam in the normal manner from the wrong side.

mark with accuracy

Accurate marking of each pattern piece makes your sewing that much easier. All those symbols and lines on the pattern tissue should be transferred to the wrong side of your fabric. They all have a separate purpose, helping you create the shape of your garment. You will know exactly where ease should be adjusted, the dart stitching lines and whether corners will match perfectly.

- Transfer the markings from your pattern pieces to the wrong side of your fabric before removing the pattern tissue. (Underlining can be marked on the right or wrong side. Pin the underlining to your fashion fabric, wrong sides together, then thread trace all necessary markings through both layers of fabric.)
- These markings serve as continuous reference points for making your garment through all stages, from pinning, stitching, fitting, to even sewing on the buttons.
- After removing the pattern tissue, transfer any position marks, foldlines or any other long lines to the right side of the fabric using thread tracing.
- Thread trace lengthwise and crosswise grainlines on the right side of the main pieces, especially if you think you will have fitting issues. These lines will help you keep the grain straight while you are adjusting the fit.

There are many weights and types of fabrics available, so you may need to use more than one method of marking. Determine the fastest, most accurate, and most appropriate way to mark your particular fabric from among the following methods.

TRACING WHEEL and **DRESSMAKER'S TRACING PAPER** are used with hard surfaced fabrics and all underlinings. Make sure that the color can be easily removed from your fabric.

- If your garment is not underlined, trace markings on the wrong side of your fabric, with the carbon side to the wrong side of your fabric.

- If your garment is underlined, mark only the underlining, not your fashion fabric.

Never use vividly contrasting colors unless you know that they will disappear during pressing or cleaning.

- To mark your fabric, insert double layers of dressmaker's carbon paper around both layers of underlining or fabric, carbon side next to the underlining or the wrong side of the fabric.

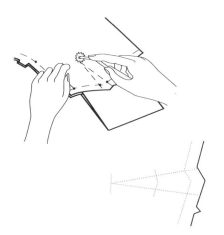

- Hold the layers in place and trace over all markings using just enough pressure to make light lines.

- Use a ruler to trace straight lines.

- Trace through the center of all the symbols. Indicate ends of darts, points of slashes, and any other symbols with short horizontal lines.

- Mark large symbols with an X.

Develop your own shorthand for marking so that you don't need to keep referring to your pattern while sewing.

TAILOR'S TACKS are used on delicate fabrics that might be marred by other marking methods. They are especially necessary for soft-surfaced fabrics, such as velvet or spongy tweeds or any fabric with a napped or nubby surface.

The technique is always the same, whether you mark the fabric as a single layer or a double layer.

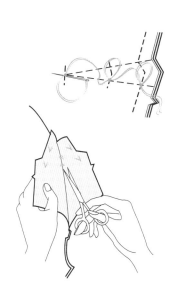

- Using a long double thread without a knot, take a single, small running stitch through your pattern tissue and fabric layers at a symbol.

- Then sew another stitch, crossing over the first, pulling the thread until a very large loop is formed.

- As you move to the next symbol, leave a loose thread between.

- Repeat the looped stitches until all symbols are marked.

- Clip the loops and threads connecting each tack.

- Carefully lift the pattern tissue off the fabric piece, roll back the upper fabric carefully and snip threads in between layers, leaving tufts on either side.

- Use pieces right away or fold carefully so that the marking threads don't slip out of position.

TAILOR'S CHALK, MARKING PENCIL or **PEN** is used on soft or hard surfaced fabrics.

- Place pins through the pattern and both layers of fabric at symbols, construction markings and corners of patterns.

- Turn the piece over and chalk the wrong side of the fabric at each pin.

- Turn the piece back to the pattern side. Starting at the edge and working toward the center, hold the pins as you remove the pattern by forcing the pinhead through the tissue and chalk the fabric.

- Remove the pins as you work.

- Run thread tracing along the chalk lines if the chalk tends to rub off.

Make sure that your pen or pencil markings will last as long as you need them. Some pen markings will disappear within 24 hours or will disappear once the piece is ironed.

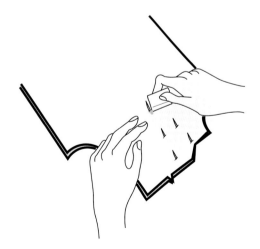 

THREAD TRACING is uneven basting for quick marking of grainlines on all garment fabrics and for transferring necessary position marks to the right side of your garment fabric. Before thread tracing, mark your pattern pieces using another method and remove tissue.

- Using a single thread, begin by taking a small backstitch. Do not knot the thread.

- Run uneven basting stitches of a size most comfortable for you, but that will be easily removable when the time comes.

- Using silk or basting thread on napped fabrics, piles and light colors to avoid leaving an imprint.

For underlining, baste corresponding pieces together and thread trace both layers. Baste within the seam allowance, not along the seam allowance. This will make threads easier to remove.

   Thread trace lengthwise grain on main pieces. Also trace the bustline, hipline, foldlines and any other construction lines necessary. For sleeves, trace the lengthwise grain from the shoulder to the elbow area and across the sleeve cap.

   By thread tracing these lines, you will see immediately any distortions caused by ill fit and they can be used as a guide for adjustments.

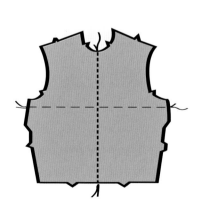
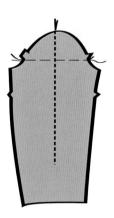
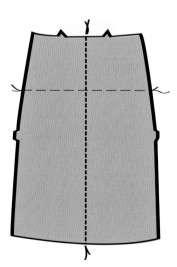

construction basics

Since making your sewing quicker and easier is our purpose, let us point out some timesaving ideas that should serve as a guide for every project you sew:

This fabric key is on every sewing guide sheet for your reference.

Right Side	Wrong Side	Interfacing	Lining	Underlining

- Do all preparatory steps first-cutting, marking, and basting the underlining to your fabric—as these operations definitely require a large, flat, clean surface that may be difficult to find once you've begun sewing.
- Apply fusible or sew-in interfacing to the required pieces all at the same time.
- Stitch as many pieces together all at one time, without cutting threads. Facings, pockets, collars, sleeves; sew from one piece right into the next.
- Then, complete sewing of small details, such as pockets, pocket flaps, and buttonholes, on each garment section before it is joined to the other sections, as the weight of the entire garment can be extremely cumbersome when you are trying to be so precise.
- Make all buttonholes at one work session to assure consistent results.
- Organize yourself by attempting to finish a complete stage of construction at each sitting.
- Spend your extra moments on those often envied finishing details such as finishing seams, attaching lingerie straps, etc.
- As a final word of professional advice, be sure to press seams as you finish each section.

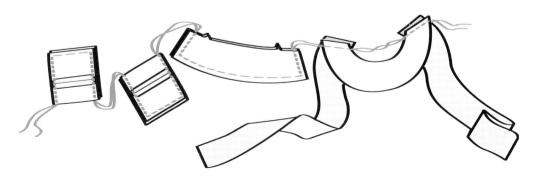

hand stitches

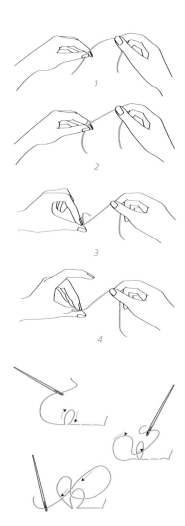

Hand sewing plays such an important part in the construction of clothes. Whether basting a seam or sewing a hem, it is the attention paid to the hand sewn details that determines the quality of your finished garment.

> Choose a needle size in accordance with your fabric and thread.

> Use a single 18" to 20" (46cm to 51cm) length of thread, coated with beeswax for added strength and slipperiness.

> Learn to wear a thimble on the second finger of your sewing hand. You'll be able to sew hard-surfaced fabrics more quickly and easily and with greater assurance.

THREADING THE NEEDLE AND KNOTTING THE THREAD:
Cut the thread at an angle; never break, bite, or tear the end; pass the cut end through the needle eye, then knot the same end you put through the eye like this:

> Using the left hand, hold the thread between the thumb and first finger (1).

> With your right hand, bring the thread over and around the fingertip, crossing it over the thread end, as shown (2).

> With your thumb over the crossed threads, and the longer thread taut, gently push the thumb toward the fingertip, causing the thread end to roll around the loop (3).

> Slide the loop off the fingertip and, lightly pinching the rolled end between the thumb and second finger, pull the longer thread in the right hand taut to set the knot (4).

FINISHING STITCHING: To end your hand stitching, you have two choices—backstitch (described later in this chapter) or a knot.

> Begin the knot by taking a tiny stitch on the wrong side of your fabric, directly over your last stitch. Pull the thread until a small loop remains.

> Run your needle through the loop, pulling the thread a second time, until another small loop is formed.

> It is through this second loop that you insert your needle for the last time. Pull the thread taut, forming an inconspicuous knot at the base of your stitches.

Basting is a temporary stitch used in the preparatory phase of your sewing. Here are some basic stitches and tips.

Always work on a flat, smooth surface. Pin your garment pieces together before basting. Use contrasting colored thread. Begin with a knot or a backstitch. Always remove basting before pressing permanent stitching. Always baste alongside the seamline within the seam allowance for easy removal of your basting threads. Silk thread is recommended for fine fabrics or when basting stitches are not to be removed before pressing, as in the case of pleats or hems.

EVEN BASTING is used for basting seams subjected to strain. It is generally used for long seams on any fabric and for areas that demand close control, such as set-in sleeves. It is usually done flat on a table, or when one layer of fabric is to be eased to the other, in the hand, with the eased layer on top. Space stitches evenly, ¼" (6mm) long and ¼" (6mm) apart, beginning and ending with backstitches rather than a knot. For firm basting, take a backstitch every few inches (centimeters). Gear the length of stitching and the type of needle to suit the fabric and probable strain.

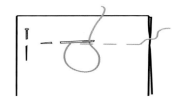

SLIP BASTING is used for matching stripes, plaids, and prints; intricate curved sections, and for fitting adjustments made from the right side. Crease and turn under the seam allowance on the edge. Right sides up, lay the folded edge in position on the corresponding piece, matching the fabric design at the seamline; pin. Slip the needle through the upper fold, then through the lower garment section, using a stitch ¼" (6mm) in length. The result is a plain seam with basting on the wrong side.

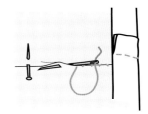

MACHINE BASTING is used for firm fabrics that won't slip or show needle marks. Set your machine for the longest stitch and loosen the upper tension slightly so thread is easily removable. To remove, clip the top thread at intervals and pull out the bobbin thread. Most brands of machine may have a built-in basting stitch.

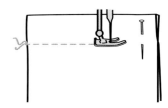

hand sewing

$H$and sewing means to stitch **_permanently_** in place by hand.

- Keep stitches fairly loose to avoid a puckered, strained look.
- Work from right to left unless otherwise stated, reversing direction if you are left-handed.
- To secure the thread in the fabric, start with a few small backstitches or make a knot at the end and conceal it in the wrong side of your fabric.

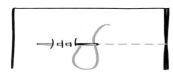

The **RUNNING STITCH** is the most basic of stitches. It has many uses—easing, gathering, tucking, mending, and sewing seams that are not subjected to much strain. Take several small forward stitches, evenly weaving the needle in and out of the fabric before pulling the thread through; pick up as many stitches as your fabric and needle will allow. For permanent seams, use stitches $1/16$" to $1/8$" (2mm to 3mm) long, for easing and gathering, $1/16$" to $1/4$" (2mm to 6mm) long.

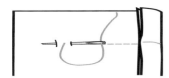

The **BACKSTITCH** is one of the strongest hand stitches. It is especially useful for repairing hard-to-reach seams that have ripped. It has the appearance of a machine stitch on the right side, but the stitches overlap on the wrong side. With right sides together, following the seam-line, bring the needle through the fabric to the upper side. Take a stitch back about $1/16$" to $1/8$" (2mm to 3mm), bringing the needle out again $1/16$" to $1/8$" (2mm to 3mm) forward on the seam-line. Keep inserting the needle in the end of the last stitch and bringing it out one stitch ahead. The stitches on the underside will be twice as long as those on the upper side.

The **PRICKSTITCH**, a variation of the backstitch, is often used for inserting zippers. The needle is carried back only one or two threads, forming a tiny surface stitch with a reinforced understitch.

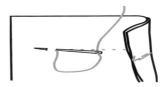

The **HAND PICKSTITCH** is used as a decorative finish and has the same appearance as the prickstitch. The only difference is that the bottom layer of fabric is not caught when backstitching. The thread should not be taut, and should lie beadlike on the fabric surface.

The **SLIPSTITCH** is used to hem, attach linings, and hold pockets and trims in place, and it provides an almost invisible finish. Slide the needle through the folded edge and at the same point pick up a thread of the under fabric. Continue in this manner, taking stitches ⅛" to ¼" (3mm to 6mm) apart; space the stitches evenly.

The **CATCHSTITCH** is used for holding two layers of fabric together in place while still maintaining a degree of flexibility. Its most common uses include attaching raw edges of facings and interfacings to the wrong side of garment sections, sewing pleats or tucks in linings, and securing hems in stretchy fabrics such as knits. Working from left to right, make a small horizontal stitch in the upper layer of fabric a short distance from the edge. Then, barely outside the edge of the upper layer, make another stitch in the lower layer of fabric diagonally across from the first stitch. Alternate stitching along the edge in a zigzag fashion, keeping threads loose.

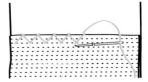

The **BLINDSTITCH**, used for hemming and holding facings in place, is inconspicuous on both sides of the garment. First, finish the raw edge of the hem or facing. Roll this edge back on the garment about ¼" (6mm); make a small horizontal stitch through one thread of the garment or underlining fabric, then pick up a thread of the hem or facing diagonally above. Do not pull the stitches tight.

The **OVERHAND STITCH** holds two finished edges together with tiny, straight, even stitches. It is primarily used to join lace edging or to attach ribbon to a garment. Insert the needle at a diagonal angle from the back edge through to the front edge, picking up only one or two threads each time.

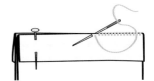

The **WHIPSTITCH** is a variation of the overhand stitch. It may serve the same purpose, differing in that the needle is inserted at a right angle to the edge, resulting in slanted stitches.

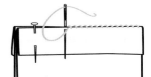

The **BLANKET STITCH** is used for a wide variety of hand-finished details. Always work from left to right with the edge of the fabric toward you. Anchor your first stitch at the edge. For the next stitch and each succeeding one, point the needle toward you and insert it through the right side of your fabric, approximately ¼" (6mm) above the edge and ¼" (6mm) over from the preceding stitch. Keep the thread below your work and under the needle, as shown. A variation of the blanket stitch is generally used to form inconspicuous thread eyes, loops, and belt carriers.

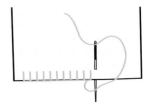

machine stitching

seams and seam finishes

Be it plain or fancy, the mark of professional sewing is a perfect seam—a seam that is never puckered, never stretched, never wobbling, and is finished without a tangle of raw or crooked edges.

- To stitch a perfect seam, always adjust the machine tension, pressure, and stitch length to suit the fabric texture and weight.
- The usual seam allowance set by the pattern industry is ⅝" (15mm) unless otherwise specified.
- If your machine doesn't have a seam guide attachment or stitching lines marked on the needle plate, place a small piece of colored tape ⅝" (15mm) from the needle as a guide.

STAYSTITCHING: Prior to pinning, basting, and permanent stitching, curved areas that require extra handling should be staystitched. This acts as a guideline for clipping and joining a curved edge to the other edges, as well as prevents stretching. Staystitch in the direction of the grain ⅛" (3mm) away from the seamline in the seam allowance, using the regular machine-stitch length suited to your fabric. For zipper openings, stitch ¼" (6mm) from the cut edge.

DIRECTIONAL STITCHING: To prevent stretching seam areas of your garment you should stitch seams in the direction of the grain just as you do when staystitching. If it is hard to tell from the cut piece which is the direction of the grain, run your finger along the edge. The threads with the grain should lie smoothly; those against will come loose and the edge will begin to fray. Without testing, you can generally stitch from the widest part to the narrowest part of each pattern piece.

constructing a seam

The main purpose of all seams is to hold your garment sections together.

JOINING SEAMLINES: When pinning the edges of your fabric together, place the pins at right angles to the seamline with the heads toward the seam allowance. It is not recommended to sew over pins. If you hit one with your needle you will most likely nick or break the needle, and you could possibly harm yourself.

STITCHING: Begin to stitch ½" (13mm) from the end, backstitch to the end, and then stitch forward. Keep stitching along the seamline, following the seam guidelines on the needle plate of your machine. Keep the cut edges of the fabric even. Secure by backstitching at the other end of the seam. Some machines have a lockstitch that may be used instead of backstitching.

The seam may also be stitched from end to end without backstitching and the ends secured by tying a knot.

REINFORCING CORNER SEAMS: Whenever you stitch a seam with a corner, use reinforcement stitches [15 to 20 per inch (6-8 per cm) depending on your fabric] to strengthen the point or inner corner.

If it is a corner that will need to be clipped for easy sewing, reinforce it before joining in a seam.

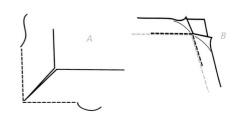

- Just inside the seamline, stitch for about an inch (25mm) on either side of the corner. Clip to the corner (A).
- Pin both sections right sides together with clipped section up and stitch, pivoting at the point (B).

To join two corresponding pieces of fabric, as in a pointed collar, reinforce while stitching the seam.

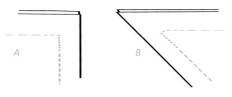

- Begin reinforcement stitches an inch (25mm) on either side of the corner (A).
- If the corner is at an acute angle, you should take one small stitch across the point for lighter-weight fabrics, and two stitches for heavier-weight fabrics (B).

TRIMMING: Seam allowances should be trimmed only where less bulk is desired.

- Enclosed seams call for ¼" (6mm) seam allowances, but if the fabric is very light you may want to trim less. Cut diagonal corners from the ends of the seams, especially if they will later cross other seams (A).
- For corners of an enclosed seam, trim across the point close to the seam. Then trim diagonally along either side of the point to eliminate any bulk when the corner is turned (B).

GRADING: When seam allowances are turned together in one direction, they must be graded to avoid making a ridge and to make seams lie flat without bulk. Grading is especially important when the fabric is heavy or if there are more than two layers of fabric. Each layer should be trimmed to a different width. Enclosed seams may be trimmed a little narrower than exposed seams. Generally the garment seam allowance is left at it's widest.

NOTCHING and CLIPPING: Curves must be graded first and then trimmed in a special way in order to lie flat. On an outward curve, cut small wedges or notches from the seam allowance at even intervals; on an inward curve, clip into the seam allowance at even intervals. These intervals should be about ½" to 1" (13mm to 25mm), depending on the sharpness of the curve. Be very careful not to clip past the seamline.

This information is at the beginning of the Sewing Instruction on the Sewing Guide Sheet included with every pattern.

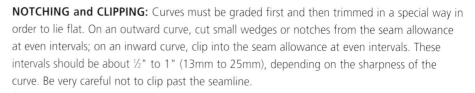

PRESSING: Pressing any seam is a two-step operation.

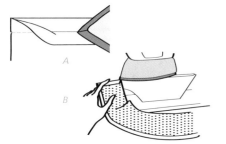

➤ First press the stitching line flat to blend the stitches into the fabric, then press the seam open. (A)

➤ For enclosed seams in collars, cuffs, and pocket flaps, before turning, press the seam open with a point presser so that the seamed edges will be sharp. Then turn and press flat. (B)

UNDERSTITCHING: When a seamline is pressed to form an edge that encloses the seam allowances, the underside should be understitched. This technique is used on facings to prevent them from rolling to the outside of the garment. Grade both seam allowances and press toward the facing. Be sure to clip or notch curved edges where necessary. From the right side of the facing, work a backstitch or machine-stitch close to the seamline and through all the seam allowances. Turn the facing in and press the seamed edge.

special seam situations

INTERSECTING or CROSSED SEAMS: Stitch one seam and press open. Stitch the second seam in the same manner. Pin the two seams with right sides together, using a point of a pin to match the crossed seams exactly at the seamline. Then pin on either side of the seams and stitch. Trim corners diagonally as shown and press remaining seam open.

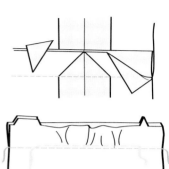

SEAM WITH EASE: To ease, stitch close to the seamline with long machine stitches extending the stitching slightly beyond markings. Pin the two layers right sides together with the eased side facing up. Pull up the ease thread between the markings and distribute the fullness evenly. Baste carefully to control the extra fabric and stitch.

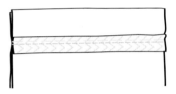

SEAM WITH GATHERS: See section on *Gathering* in this chapter.

TAPING A SEAM: A seam may be stayed or taped to strengthen and prevent stretching in the finished garment by using twill tape, woven seam binding or clear elastic tape. This technique is often used at waistline and shoulder seams. The tape should be placed over the seamline of one garment section, with the edge extending ⅛" (3mm) into the seam allowance. Baste next to the seamline and sew the tape on permanently as the seam is machine-stitched.

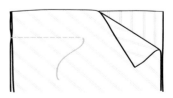

Use clear elastic to stay shoulder seams of knits.

TISSUE PAPER UNDER SEAMS: Some lightweight fabrics are inclined to stretch or shift during sewing, creating uneven seams. To prevent mishaps, try placing tissue paper on the machine bed under the seams. Stitch through both the fabric and the paper, then tear the paper away. Tear-away stabilizers in various weights are available for the same purpose.

BIAS-CUT SEAMS: If you are joining a bias edge to a straight edge, pin and baste the bias edge to the straight edge. When stitching, be sure to always keep the bias side up in order to control the stretch of the bias and to avoid puckers.

If you are joining two bias edges, stretch the fabric slightly as you stitch over tissue paper so that the finished edge will hang correctly. Otherwise the seam may pucker and the threads will break when the garment is worn.

If it is a lengthwise seam, baste the fabric together, and let the garment hang for 24 hours to allow the bias to stretch before stitching the seam.

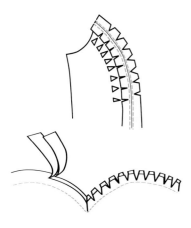

PRINCESS SEAM: Staystitch both curved edges ⅛" (3mm) from the seamline within the seam allowance. Clip the inward curved seam allowance on the center panel of the garment to the staystitching. Pin the seamline, spreading the clipped edge so that it will lie smoothly. Make any additional clips if necessary. With clipped side up, stitch the two edges together, being careful to keep the underside smooth. Press seam open over a tailor's ham, notching the seam allowance on the side panel until it lies flat. Wherever possible, stagger the position of the clips and notches.

SCALLOPS: Stitch the curved scallop seam with small reinforcement stitches [15-20 per inch (6-8 per cm)]. Take one stitch across each point to make turning easier later. Now clip into each point, being careful not to cut through the stitching. Grade the seams and notch all the curves.

seam finishes

A seam finish helps the seam allowances to support the garment shape, ensures durability, prevents raveling, and contributes to the overall neatness of the garment.

MACHINE ZIGZAG or STRAIGHT STITCH: For fabrics that tend to ravel easily, use a zigzag or straight stitch to reinforce each raw edge. Use a smaller stitch for lightweight fabrics and a larger stitch for heavy, bulky fabrics, pre-testing for the best results.

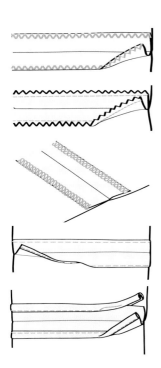

PINKED: If you are working with a firmly woven fabric that does not ravel, pink the edges with pinking or scalloping shears. For an even more secure finish, you may wish to stitch ¼" (6mm) from each edge before you begin to pink.

SERGED OR OVERLOCKED: This edge finish is appropriate for nearly all fabrics, as it can be sewn in a 2- or 3-thread (or more) configuration depending on the weight of the fabric. The machine trims the fabric while it finishes the edges.

TURNED UNDER: Use this method for lightweight fabrics and plain-weave synthetics. It is not suitable for fabrics with bulk. Turn under the raw edges of the seam allowances, press if necessary, and stitch close to the edge.

BOUND EDGE: For heavy, bulky, easily frayed fabrics, especially in unlined jackets or coats, encase each raw edge in purchased double-fold bias tape. Use purchased tricot tape or strips of organza on lace or other lightweight fabrics.

self-finished seams

Some seaming techniques enclose the seam allowances as the seam is stitched. This gives a very neat appearance to seams that are visible such as in sheer fabrics and in unlined jackets.

FRENCH SEAM: This seam is well suited to sheer fabrics. It looks like a plain seam on the right side and a small, neat tuck on the wrong side. It is used on straight seams. Pin wrong sides together and stitch ⅜" (10mm) from the seamline in the seam allowance. Trim to within ⅛" to ¼" (3mm to 6mm) of stitching. With right sides together, crease along the stitched seam; press. Stitch along the seamline, encasing the raw edges.

FLAT-FELL SEAM: A sturdy seam often used on sportswear and menswear. With wrong sides together, stitch a plain seam, and press toward one side. Trim the lower seam allowance to ⅛" (3mm). Turn under the edge of the other seam allowance ¼" (6mm) and fold over the narrow seam allowance. For non-bulky fabrics, machine-stitch close to the folded edge; for bulky reversible fabrics, slipstitch the fold in place. Many machines have feller feet to guide the fabric in stitching this seam.

SELF-BOUND SEAM: Trim one seam allowance of a plain seam to ⅛" or ¼" (3mm or 6mm), depending on your fabric. Turn the edge of the other seam allowance under and slipstitch or machine-stitch over the seam, encasing the trimmed seam allowance.

HAIRLINE SEAM: For sheer fabrics where there is no strain, place a narrow row of zigzag stitching along the seamline, then trim away the seam allowances as close to the stitching as possible.

DOUBLE-STITCHED SEAM: This seam can be used on soft knits that have a tendency to curl at the edges. Stitch a plain seam, then stitch again ⅛" (3mm) away within the seam allowance using either a straight stitch or a narrow zigzag stitch. Trim seam allowances close to stitching.

OVERLOCK SEAM: An overlock machine or serger sews the seam and trims the fabric all at the same time. These seams are good for knits but are also suitable for wovens.

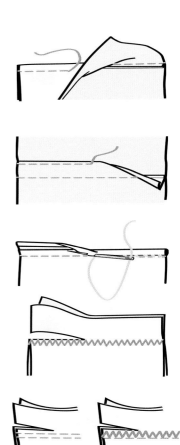

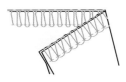

decorative seams

You can be creative in your sewing by letting your seams show. Choose one of these stitch techniques as a design feature for your garment and be inventive-your finished product will be an original!

TOPSTITCHED SEAM: Press a plain seam to one side as indicated on the pattern instructions. Topstitch the desired distance from the seam on the right side of the fabric through all thicknesses.

DOUBLE TOPSTITCHED SEAM: First press a plain seam open. Topstitch the desired distance from each side of the seam on the right side of the fabric. Be sure your stitches go through both thicknesses of the fabric.

WELT SEAM: Stitch a plain seam and press it toward one side. Trim the inner seam allowance to ¼" (6mm). Then stitch through the upper seam allowance and garment, encasing the inner seam allowance.

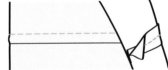

DOUBLE WELT SEAM: When completed, this seam gives much the same appearance as a flat-fell seam. First construct a welt seam as directed above. Then, stitch close to the seam on the right side of the fabric, as shown.

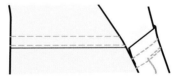

LAPPED SEAM: Turn in the edges of the overlapping section along the seamline and press. Working from the right side, pin the folded edge over the remaining section with the fold along the seamline. Stitch close to the fold through all thicknesses.

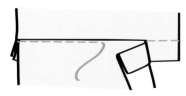

constructing a basic dart

- Mark your dart position using a tracing wheel and tracing paper, tailor's chalk or tailor's tacks.
- Match the symbols and pin.
- Stitch along the dart line, shortening your stitch length ½" (13mm) from pointed end to 12-14 stitches per inch (25mm).
- Sew off end of point, leaving a thread tail.
- DO NOT BACK STITCH AT POINT. Tie off thread ends in a knot and trim excess thread.

To achieve a smooth point at the end of the dart, decrease the length of your stitches as you near the point. This secures the threads without having to tie a knot.

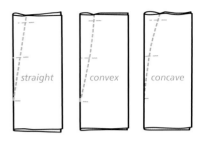

straight *convex* *concave*

pressing

Press darts as you are sewing before stitching any seams through the darts. Press vertical darts towards centers. Horizontal darts are usually pressed down. Press darts flat, being careful not to crease fabric beyond the dart point. If desired, press darts over a curved surface such as a tailor's ham or press mitt to maintain the built in space.

Place a piece of brown paper between the garment and the dart and press. This will prevent the dart shadow from showing on the outside of your garment.

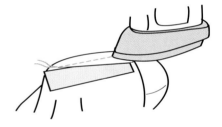

trimming

Most darts will only need pressing. Deep darts on medium to heavy fabrics will need to be slashed to within ½" (13mm) from the point and pressed open.

Darts in sheer fabrics will look better if they are trimmed. Make a second row of stitching about ⅛" (3mm) from the first stitching, Trim close to second stitching and machine zigzag to finish edge.

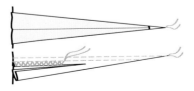

French dart

The French dart is a long curved dart that begins at the side seam and extends diagonally from the hip to the bust. Sometimes the center of the dart is trimmed out on the pattern.

▶ Trace all dart lines and mark the matching points.

▶ Staystitch ⅛" (3mm) inside the dart stitching line.

▶ Pin stitching lines together matching corresponding markings. Stitch dart.

▶ Slash dart to within ¼" (6mm) of point and clip seam allowances to allow dart to curve. Press.

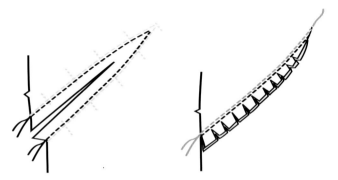

contour dart

The contour dart tapers upward to the bust or back and downward to the hip.

▶ Mark all dart lines and stitching lines.

▶ Fold the dart along the centerline and pin stitching lines together.

▶ Starting from the center, the widest part of the dart, stitch toward each point. Knot thread ends at points.

▶ Clip dart at waistline and at several other points along the fold so dart will lie flat when pressed. Press darts towards center.

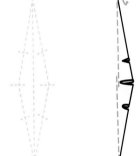

tucks

There are three commonly known types of tucks: BLIND TUCKS, where each tuck touches or overlaps the next, SPACED TUCKS, where there is a predetermined space between each tuck, and PIN TUCKS, which are very narrow spaced tucks.

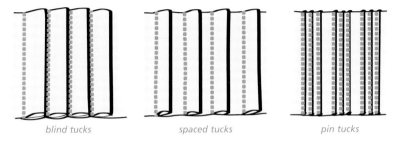

blind tucks   *spaced tucks*   *pin tucks*

making uniform tucks

Tucks are usually made on the straight grain. Do be sure to make the fold of the tucks parallel to the threads in the fabric.

MARKING and BASTING: Mark stitching lines of each tuck on either the outside or inside of your fabric. Remove the pattern, fold the tucks either to the inside or outside of the garment, matching stitching lines. Baste in place.

Or eliminate marking your tucks by making a cardboard measurement gauge, cutting a notch for the depth of the tuck and a second notch to indicate the space from fold to fold.

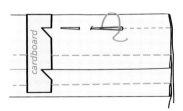

- Place the top of the gauge along the fold of the first tuck.
- Using the first notch as a guide, make a row of basting stitches parallel to the fold, sliding the gauge as you stitch.
- For the next tuck, move the gauge so that the second notch is now even with the first fold, and make your next fold at the top of the gauge.
- Continue this procedure for each consecutive tuck.

A louvered pleating board or stainless steel pleating bar are two very handy tools that help you mark and press even tucks or pleats into your fabric before stitching.

Construction Basics   59

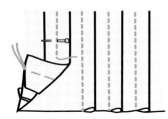

STITCHING: To control the finished look and the evenness of the stitching, be sure to stitch from the side of the tuck that will be seen.

- For narrow tucks, from ¼ to ¾ (6mm to 20mm) wide, you can use the needle plate on your machine as a guide for stitching.
- Use the quilting bar attached to your machine or presser foot for wider tucks.
- Tucking may be pieced, if necessary, by carefully lapping, then stitching the tucks.

PRESSING: Press tucks as you stitch each one, or directly after stitching the series.

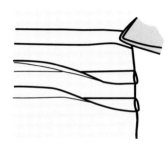

- First press the crease in the tuck from the right side of your fabric but on the underneath side of the fold. This step makes the final pressing much easier.
- Press the entire tucked area from the wrong side. Use very little steam to prevent puckering or the tuck fold from making unwanted indentations in the fabric.
- To prevent unwanted indentations in some fabrics, use strips of brown paper under the fold of each tuck as you press.
- Touch up the right side of the tucks as necessary.

RELEASED TUCKS or **DART TUCKS** may have fullness released at one or both ends of the tuck. Construction techniques will vary greatly according to where the tuck is located on the garment.

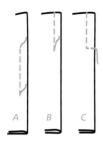

- Regardless of construction, the most significant factor to remember about all released tucks is that the released fullness above and below the stitched fold should never be pressed flat. (A)
- The stitching line at the point of releasing fullness can be backstitched, or the thread ends tied securely. (B)
- When the tucks are pressed to one side, stitch across to the fold and backstitch or knot the thread ends. (C)

There are four well known variations, used either singly or in a series: KNIFE or SIDE PLEATS with all folds turned to one side; BOX PLEATS with two folds turned away from each other and under folds meeting at the center; INVERTED PLEATS, box pleats in reverse, with folds turned toward each other and meeting; and ACCORDION PLEATS, always pressed along the entire length with folds resembling the bellows of an accordion.

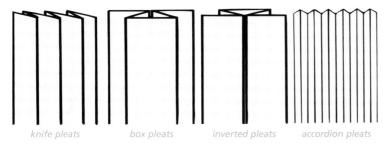

| *knife pleats* | *box pleats* | *inverted pleats* | *accordion pleats* |

straight pleats

Pleat on a surface large enough to hold the entire pleated garment. For multiple pleats, complete the hem before making the pleat folds. Your length can be adjusted from the waistline after the pleats are formed.

MARKING: Pleats can be made either from the right or wrong side, depending upon the method that works best for you. Whichever method you choose, be sure to transfer your markings to the right side of the fabric when forming pleats on the right side, or to the wrong side when pleating on the wrong side of the fabric.

Use different colors of thread to key the various "line" indications.

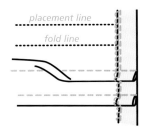

placement line

fold line

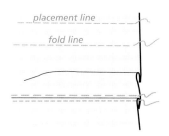

placement line

fold line

PLEATING: Pressed and unpressed pleats are both made the same way; pressing makes the difference.

From the wrong side:

- Bring the indicated markings for each pleat together and baste.
- Press or turn pleats in the direction indicated for your type of pleat.
- Baste pleats in place along waistline edge.

From the right side:

- Following your markings, turn the fabric in along foldline or roll line.
- Bring the edge to the placement line and pin.
- Starting at the hem edge and working upward, baste each pleat in place through all thicknesses.
- Baste pleats in place along waistline edge.

PRESSING: For pressed pleats, make certain the pleats are accurately measured, marked, and basted.

- Pin them to the ironing board at the edge and steam them on both sides just enough to set them.
- Use a press cloth on the right side to avoid shine.
- Support overhanging fabric by a chair or table to prevent the weight of the fabric from pulling the pleats out of shape.

If you discover that light pressing creates an unattractive ridge or line on your fabric, insert strips of brown paper or even envelopes under the fold of the pleat before you press.

To assure yourself of a sharp, lasting press, iron on both sides of the pleats. Unpressed pleats may require a very slight steaming just to set the shape and fall of the pleat as the designer intended. This can be done most effectively as the garment hangs on your dress form.

shaped and stitched pleats

These pleats are most frequently used to reduce bulk in the hip area by trimming away the upper portion of the pleat, leaving a ⅝" (15mm) seam allowance along the stitched seamline.

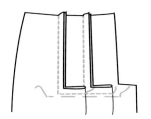

- Join all skirt sections together. Start pleats 6" to 8" (15cm to 20.5cm) from the lower edge (to allow for hemming later), and bring the indicated pleat and/or seamlines together following markings; baste.
- Before stitching, try the garment on to see if adjustments are needed.
- When the necessary adjustments are completed, stitch along the indicated seamlines from the bottom upward.
- Complete the hem and baste remainder of pleats into place before pressing.

With this type of construction, a stay of lining fabric may be needed to support the upper edge of the pleats. Use the stay pattern pieces or on the straight grain, shape a stay to fit into the desired area. Baste the upper edge to the pleated area at the waistline; then turn under and slipstitch the lower edge of the stay over the upper edge of the pleats along the seamlines.

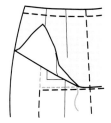

On inverted box pleats, a self-stay can be formed by trimming away only half of the top of the pleat, leaving a seam allowance of ⅝" (15mm). The remaining pleat fabric can then be basted across the upper edge for support.

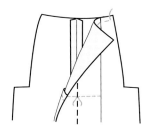

pleats with a separate underlay

These pleats are made from the inside and are often used singly.

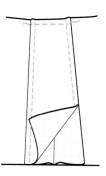

- Bring the coordinating markings together and baste. Open out the pleat extensions.
- Stitch the pleat underlay to the pleat extensions and baste in place across the upper edge. Press the seam allowances flat, not open.
- Check the fit for necessary adjustments.
- Then join all seams and prepare your hem.

edgestitching and topstitching

When you are certain that your pleats fit and hang properly, are well pressed, and are hemmed evenly, the folds can be edgestitched to keep creases sharp. The pleats can also be held in place by topstitching through all thicknesses from the hip area to the waist. Both edgestitching and topstitching should be done before the skirt is permanently attached to the garment or waistband.

EDGESTITCHING STRAIGHT PLEATS: Stitch close to the outside creased edge of each pleat from the hem up toward the waistline. You may also want to stitch the inside folds on the wrong side. Your edgestitching foot is ideal for straight stitching. Pull thread ends to inside and tie.

TOPSTITCHING STRAIGHT PLEATS: Always stitch on the right side of the garment, through all thicknesses, from the hip area to the waist. Mark each pleat where the topstitching will begin.

- For knife or side pleats, stitch along the fold upward to the waist. (A)
- For inverted pleats, topstitching is done on both sides of the pleat. Make 2 or 3 stitches across the pleat, pivot, and stitch along the fold to the waist. Repeat on other side of pleat. (B)
- Pull thread ends to inside and tie.

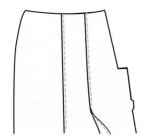

EDGESTITCHING SHAPED PLEATS: Release the stitching for about 1" (25mm) at the hipline of each pleat. Edgestitch the creased edge of each pleat on the outside from the hem to the hipline. Connecting stitches, edgestitch along the seam through all thicknesses from the hipline to the waistline. Pull the thread ends to the inside and tie.

A godet can be used to add flounce to a sleeve and swing to a skirt. It can be a pie-shaped, semi-circular, rectangular, or pleated piece of fabric set into a seam, dart, cutout, or slash to give extra width to a hem. The pie-shaped godet is the most common shape. It is usually cut with the straight grain down the center of the fabric, leaving bias edges on the sides.

inserting the godet

IN A SLASH:

- Reinforce the slash by sewing just inside the seamlines in the seam allowance, using small stitches [15-20 per inch (6-8 per cm)] on both sides of the point and pivoting at the point.

- If fabric is especially fragile, reinforce point with a patch of underlining on the right side of the fabric. At the point, clip exactly to stitching.

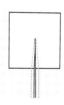

- Pin godet to slash, turning the patch inside and matching the godet marking to the clipped point first.

- Baste and stitch, slashed side up, from point to hem. Press seams toward garment.

IN A SEAM OR DART:

- Stitch the seam or dart to the marking; pull threads through and tie securely. For heavy or stretchy fabrics, center ribbon seam binding over seamlines for support.

- Pin godet to garment, matching seamlines and markings. Baste and stitch on either side from point to hem. Press godet flat.

- If inserted into dart, clip godet seam allowance to seam. Press seam allowances open below the clip, toward the garment above the clip, and open again above the point.

With heavy or loosely woven fabrics, stitch the godet to the garment for only a few inches (centimeters) on either side of the point and let the remainder of the godet hang free for 24 hours to allow the bias to set. Before hemming, allow all garments to hang 24 hours.

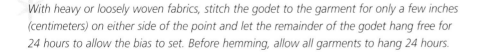

Gathers are small, soft folds made by drawing fabric up on a line of hand or machine stitching. In order to have small, even folds when stitching for gathering, do not use a longer stitch than necessary. First, try approximately 8 stitches per inch (3 per cm). If the fabric still does not gather easily, lengthen the stitch accordingly. Normally, thick and closely woven fabrics need longer stitches than lightweight and sheer fabrics.

how to gather

Method 1

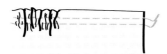

➤ With the right side of the fabric up, stitch along the seamline and again ¼" (6mm) away in the seam allowance.

➤ To form the gathers, pin the edge to be gathered to the corresponding shorter edge at notches, centers, and all remaining markings. Draw up the bobbin threads at one end until almost half of the gathered edge fits the adjoining straight edge.

➤ Fasten gathers by winding threads around a pin in a figure-eight fashion. Draw up the remaining half and again fasten the threads. Adjust gathers evenly between pins; then stitch on the seamline with the gathered side up.

➤ Press the seam, taking care not to flatten the gathers, and then lightly press in the desired direction.

Thread your bobbin with heavy-duty thread or buttonhole twist to help prevent the thread from breaking when you pull up the gathering.

When you are using a gathering stitch on heavy, bulky fabrics, try to avoid stitching across your seam allowances. When applying your gathering stitch, stitch up to the seamline and stop; then begin on the other side of the seamline.

Method 2

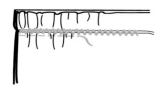

➤ Thread a narrow cord, gimp or buttonhole twist under the back of your all purpose presser foot and up and through the front for easy guiding.

➤ Using a wide zigzag stitch, stitch over the cord being careful not to stitch into it.

➤ Pull up the gathers and stitch along the seam line just below the cord.

➤ Remove cord when the seam is completed.

Method 3

➤ Gathering by hand is done with small, even running stitches, the same length on both sides of the fabric. Sew at least two rows.

➤ For hand gathering it is best to work on an individual fabric piece before the pieces are joined to each other. (Not shown)

STAYING GATHERS: Seam binding or twill tape can be used as a stay to reinforce and finish off a gathered seam. Place seam binding or tape with one edge right next to the seam line, and stitch along lower edge through all thicknesses.

ruffles

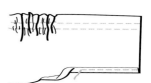

There are two types of ruffles: the straight ruffle, whose fullness is created by gathering a rectangular strip of fabric; and the circular ruffle, whose fullness is created when the inner curve of the circle is straightened.

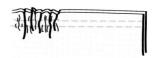

straight ruffles

A straight ruffle is gathered and constructed from a continuous strip of material. It can be cut either on the straight grain or on the bias. If the ruffle must be seamed, the seam should be made on the straight grain. Bias ruffles applied to a small area are the exception.

A straight ruffle may be constructed of a single layer of fabric with a narrow hem at the lower edge. Or the ruffle may be self-faced by folding the fabric in half lengthwise with wrong sides together.

For gathering a ruffle, always stitch two rows of long machine stitches-one on the seamline and the other ¼" (6mm) away in the seam allowance. Review *Gathering* section for how-to's.

Draw the gathers to the proper length, adjust, and stitch to your garment. Finish seam, following the pattern instructions.

double ruffle

A variation of the straight ruffle, the double ruffle has two long edges and is gathered in the center.

▶ Make a narrow hem along the two free edges. The fabric can be doubled for a self-facing, having the raw edges meet directly under the gathering line. If the ends will be left hanging free, finish with a narrow hem, or seam and trim ends that are to be joined.

▶ Stitch along ruffle gathering lines indicated on the pattern. Draw up gathers and adjust ruffle length.

▶ To apply the ruffle to a finished edge, pin it wrong side down on the right side of the garment. Baste, adjusting the gathers to fit.

▶ Topstitch twice, stitching close to both rows of gathering stitches. Remove gathering stitches, if desired.

ruffle with a heading

When the ruffle is gathered off-center it's called a ruffle with a heading. This can be applied in the same way as a double ruffle.

circular ruffle

A circular ruffle can be added to any edge—cuffs, V-neckline, rounded neckline—wherever you wish. It is cut from several circles that are first slashed and then joined along the straight grain. Carefully lay out, pin, and cut the ruffle sections. The exact location and maintenance of the grainline is most important if the circular ruffle is to drape correctly.

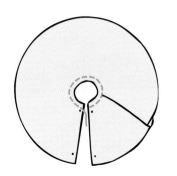

Create Ruffle

▶ Staystitch each ruffle section ⅛" (3mm) from the inner seamline in the seam allowance before joining.

▶ The edge of a circular ruffle may be faced with self-fabric or it may have a narrow hemmed or rolled serger edge.

▶ If your ruffle requires a hem, join the circles and complete the hem before basting the ruffle to its proper edge.

▶ If your ruffle has a facing of corresponding circles, stitch the seamed facing and ruffle sections together along the outer edges. Trim seam allowance to ¼" (6mm). Turn the ruffle and press. Baste the raw edges of the ruffle and facing together for handling ease.

Applying ruffles to a neckline or any other curved edge:

- Staystitch the garment seamline so that its shape will not be distorted by the weight of the ruffle.
- Clip the staystitched edge where necessary as you pin the ruffle to the garment in order to fit smoothly on the seamline.
- As a rule, deep curves require a clip at almost every ½" (13mm) up to the line of staystitching; shallow curves will require fewer clips.
- If the ruffle does not lie flat, do not cut through the staystitching; merely clip more frequently.
- Baste the ruffle in place.

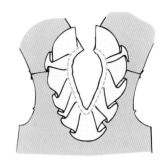

finishing ruffles

SHAPED FACING: For ruffles sewn into a facing, pin the facing to the garment edge over your ruffle.

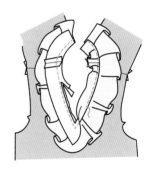

- The ruffle is now sandwiched between the two layers, right sides together. Stitch along the seamline.
- Trim, grade, and clip the seam allowance so that the facing will lie flat when turned.
- Turn the facing to expose the finished ruffle. Press, being careful not to press over the ruffle.
- Understitch the facing by hand or machine through all thicknesses to prevent it from rolling to the outside.
- If you are using a zipper, insert your zipper and slipstitch the facing along the zipper tape. Blindstitch the facing to the garment or underlining or tack in place at shoulders.

ENCASED IN A SEAM: Pin the matching garment section to your garment over the ruffle. Follow the instructions for Shaped Facing to complete construction.

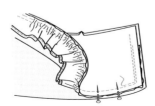

BIAS FACING: For a fine finish on ruffles at a hemline, cut a bias strip of your fashion fabric, or a firm, lightweight fabric, 1¼" (3.2cm) wide and ½" (13mm) longer than the length of the seam to be faced.

- Stitch a ¼" (6mm) seam at the short ends of the strip.
- With the raw-edges even, pin the bias strip over the basted ruffle.
- Then stitch a ⅝" (15mm) seam through all thicknesses, trim, and if necessary, grade the seam allowances.
- Turn the bias to the inside and press. Turn the raw edge under ¼" (6mm) and slipstitch or machine stitch it to the garment or underlining.

mitering

Mitering is a neat and easy means of eliminating bulk at corners. Most miters involve folds, either at right angles or 45° angles to the area being mitered. The method you use to miter depends on many factors—whether you are working with garment areas, binding, or continuous strips of trim, and whether the miter is made as you attach the trim or before application.

continuous strips

If your band or trim has seam allowances, press them to the inside before you begin mitering.

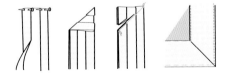

- To miter the band before it is applied, pin the band to the garment for an accurate measurement of where the miter should be made.
- Measure to the outermost point where the corner will be formed, and mark with a pin.
- Remove band and fold it with right sides together at marked point.
- Turn the fold diagonally to meet the turned-back edges of band, as shown, and press.
- Open the diagonal fold and stitch along the pressed crease. Since it is important that the knots do not show once the miter is finished, pull the thread ends to one side of the band and knot. Trim to ⅛" (3mm) and press the seam open.
- Attach the strip.

trim

To miter while you are attaching trim, use trim with a finished edge such as ribbon or braid.

- Pin the trim in position, then edgestitch or hand-sew the inner edge.
- Fold the band back on itself, then diagonally to the side, making a right angle; press.
- Again fold the band back on itself and stitch on the diagonal crease-through the band and garment. Since it is important that the knots be invisible once the miter is finished, pull the thread ends to one side of the band and knot.
- If trim is bulky, you may trim the small corner close to the stitching.
- Press flat from the right side; miter remaining corners, and edgestitch or hand-sew outer edge in place.

square corners

Pockets, appliqués, or any other applied areas requiring square corners, need to be mitered so the excess fullness can be easily trimmed away. Pressing is the key feature.

Method 1:

- Turn all seam allowances to inside and press.
- At the corners, open the seam allowances and turn them to the inside diagonally across the point, and press.
- Trim corner to ⅜" (10mm) from the pressed diagonal crease.
- Slipstitch to fasten miter.

Method 2:

- For a quick sturdier method, make a diagonal fold in the turned-back seam allowances at the corners and press.
- Stitch along the pressed diagonal crease.
- Trim the seam diagonally to ⅜" (10mm) or less for bulkier fabrics, as shown.
- Press diagonal seam open, then turn the corners to the inside. Press.

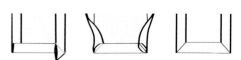

construction techniques

interfacing applications

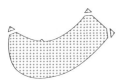

fusible interfacing

Fusible interfacings require the proper combination of steam, heat, and pressure for a specific amount of time in order to achieve a lasting bond. Follow the manufacturer's instructions precisely, and pretest on a scrap of your fabric before beginning to fuse. Check the crispness of the fused sample—the fusing process sometimes adds a little body or stiffness to the fabric.

Fusible interfacings are usually applied directly to the facing. It makes finishing the edge much easier and more stable. For small detail areas, such as cuffs and pocket flaps, fusible interfacings are applied to the outer fabric sections.

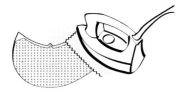

▷ Cut out fusible interfacing, being sure grainline or stretch direction is positioned as you desire. Trim diagonally at any corners to further reduce bulk. Trim away seam allowances to reduce bulk for heavier-weight fusible interfacings, you may wish to trim away the entire seam allowance.

▷ Place interfacing with adhesive side down against wrong side of fabric, aligning seamlines. Hold in position by steam basting, pressing lightly with the tip of your iron in several places.

▷ To fuse, press down firmly using a steam iron and/or damp press cloth for 10 to 15 seconds, depending on manufacturer's directions. Press one area, then lift up iron and press again, overlapping the previous area. Do not slide iron along fabric or you may form wrinkles.

▷ Turn the piece over and, using a press cloth, repeat the fusing process again from the right side of the fabric.

Most fusible interfacings can be removed by repressing until the two layers of fabric can be pulled apart, but the interfacing cannot be refused.

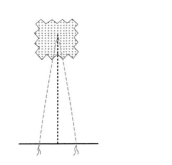

Fusible interfacings can be used to stabilize areas such as buttonholes, slashes, and plackets. If the interfacing edge creates a visible outline on the right side of the fabric, pink the edges of the interfacing before fusing.

fusing agents

Fusible web is used to hold two layers of fabrics together. Use in detail areas such as hems, cuffs, pocket flaps, and belts to add body by fusing the layers of fabric together. Unlike interfacing, fusing agents cannot be used to stabilize areas to prevent stretching.

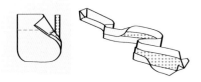

sew-in interfacing

Two different methods can be used for stitching interfacing to a garment, depending on the weight of the interfacing fabric. Light and medium weight interfacings have very little bulk so they can be stitched into the seams. Heavier weight interfacings and all hair canvases are too bulky or rigid to extend past the seamline, so trim the seam allowances away before the interfacing is attached.

Interfacing is usually cut from the facing pattern pieces. Separate interfacing pieces are provided for tailored jackets and coats that have a large portion of the garment interfaced. Follow your pattern directions for the correct placement of the interfacing on the garment sections.

LIGHT AND MEDIUM WEIGHT INTERFACING

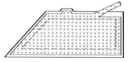

- Cut out the interfacing, being sure that the pattern pieces are placed correctly if interfacing has grainlines or stretchability.
- Pin interfacing to wrong side of fabric, matching seamlines and markings. Baste next to the seamline in the seam allowance, or stitch ½" (13mm) from the edge.

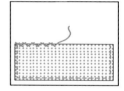

- Trim interfacing close to stitching. Stitch seams; trim and grade fabric seam allowances.

On a garment section with a foldline along one edge, such as a collar, cuff, or waistband, the interfacing should be trimmed at the foldline if the edge will be topstitched or edgestitched. Catchstitch the interfacing to the garment along the foldline.

For a softly rounded edge, extend the interfacing approximately ½" (13mm) beyond the foldline. Secure interfacing to garment along the foldline with long running stitches spaced about ½" (13mm) apart.

HEAVY WEIGHT INTERFACING

Cut out interfacing, checking on pattern placement as for light and medium weight interfacings. Stitch any darts or center back collar seam in the interfacing.

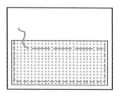

- Trim away all seam allowances. Pin interfacing to wrong side of fabric, aligning cut edges of interfacing with seamlines of the garment; baste in place.
- Catchstitch interfacing to the garment along seamlines.

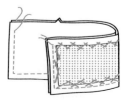

- Pin, baste, and stitch interfaced garment sections together.

To attach interfacing along a foldline, use either catchstitches or long running stitches as shown previously.

facings

A well-applied facing does much for the look and comfort of your new garment. The purpose of a facing is to neatly finish and conceal a raw edge by turning it to the wrong side of your garment. There are three basic facing categories—a **shaped facing**, an **extended facing**, or a **bias facing**.

Finish the raw edge of the facing by stitching ¼" (6mm) from the unnotched edge, trim to ⅛" (3mm) and zigzag or overcast with your serger.

For a more attractively finished appearance, try enclosing the edges with bias binding, stretch lace, or other lightweight, flexible trims.

When the facing is attached, press the seam or foldlines carefully before you turn and tack the facings to the inside of the garment. To prevent the facing from rolling to the outside, open out the facing and understitch it to the seam allowances. If the facing edge is at a visible area, you can favor the garment slightly along the seamline so that the facing does not show. This means that the outside of the garment is rolled very slightly to the inside, so that the facing seam won't show when worn.

Tack the facing to the inside of the garment to keep it in place. Tack loosely; many short, tight stitches will give your garment a strained or puckered appearance. Blindstitch the facing to the underlining.

Don't forget the facings if you have to make any adjustments or alterations to your pattern.

shaped facing

A shaped or fitted facing is the most commonly selected method used to finish necklines and sleeveless armholes.

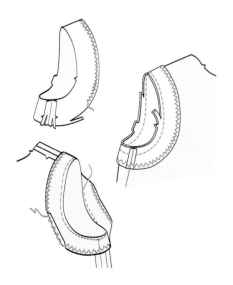

➤ Prepare the facing by applying interfacing, if indicated by the pattern, stitching, trimming, and pressing the seams. Finish the outer edge.

➤ Pin the facing to the garment, matching the seams and markings. Then, with the facing side up, stitch the facing to the garment. Trim, grade, and clip the seam allowances. Press the seam allowances toward the facing.

➤ To keep the facing from rolling to the outside, open out the facing and understitch it to the seam allowances, pulling it taut as you stitch.

➤ Turn the facing to the inside and press. Tack the facing to the inner seams, or blindstitch the free edge to the underlining.

For a neckline facing with a zipper opening, insert the zipper first, then attach the facing.

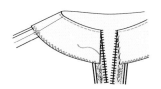

- Turn the facing ends under to clear the zipper teeth and slipstitch the ends in place.
- Tack the facing at the shoulder seams or blindstitch facing edge to underlining. Fasten with a hook and eye at top of placket, if desired.

stay the seamline

When working with soft or loosely woven fabrics that tend to stretch, stabilize the garment edge with ribbon seam binding. Necklines that are cut on the bias must also be reinforced to prevent stretching of the curved or bias edge.

Center the seam binding over the seamline on the inside of your garment, folding out any fullness at points or corners and baste in place. Finish applying the facing according to your pattern directions.

combination facings

This is a variation of the shaped facing in which the neckline and armhole facings are cut and applied as one piece. It is often used on garments with narrow shoulder seams, such as a dress with cutaway armholes. **Do not sew the shoulder seams of either the garment or the facing until after the facing is stitched to the garment.**

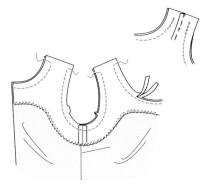

- Join the garment sections at the side seams, leaving the shoulder seams open, and press. Join the facing sections together in the same manner and press. Then, finish the unnotched facing edge as desired.
- Prior to pinning the facing to the garment, pin a minute tuck in both garment shoulders, as shown. This ensures that the seams and facing will not show on the right side once the facing is turned.
- Pin the facing to the garment, right sides together. Since the raw edges will not be even, follow the seamline of the facing. Stitch to within ⅝" (15mm) from shoulder edges and backstitch. Grade and clip seam allowances. Unpin the tuck in the garment shoulders. Turn the facing to the inside and press.

- To prevent the facing from rolling out, understitch to the seam allowances close to the seam. Fold the facing seam allowances back and stitch the garment shoulder seams, carefully keeping the facing free.
- Trim and press open the garment seams. (Tie off threads so they won't show.) Turn in the facing edges and slipstitch them together over the garment seam. On bulky fabric, trim the facing seam allowance to ¼" (6mm) before turning in.

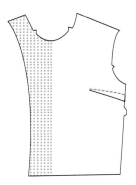

extended facing

An extended facing is cut in one piece with the garment and folded to the inside. It is used for finishing edges cut on straight grain that can simply be extended to create a fold at the edge rather than a seam.

Because extended facing edges are usually overlapped, be sure to mark center lines and other markings. Interface for reinforcement, especially if a buttonhole closing is intended.

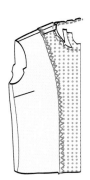

- Apply the interfacing to the garment self-facing.
- If additional facing sections are to be joined to the extended facing, such as the back neck facing, attach these sections before stitching the facing to the garment.
- Finish raw edges.
- Turn facing to the right side along the foldline of the garment so right sides are together. If a collar is part of the design, this should be completed and pinned to the neck edge first.
- Pin the facing to the garment along the neck seamline. Stitch the seam; trim, grade, and clip the seam allowances.
- Turn the facing to the inside and press. Understitch close to the neckline seam through the facing and the seam allowances. Tack the facing in place at the shoulder seams.

bias facing

Ease of handling and versatility make a bias facing a suitable replacement for your regular shaped facing. It is particularly useful when you do not want to use your garment fabric (if it is scratchy or bulky) or where a wide facing may be objectionable (as in sheers). Bias strips can be cut from your fashion fabric, lining or underlining.

- Cut a bias strip four times the desired width plus ¼" to ⅜" (6mm to 10mm) to allow for shaping (or use double-fold bias tape with folds pressed open) and the length of the garment edge plus 2" (5cm) to allow for finishing the ends.
- Fold the strip in half lengthwise with wrong sides together. Press the strip lightly, steaming and stretching it into curves corresponding to those of the garment edge.
- Your closure should be completed before you apply your bias facing. If you have a zipper, trim the zipper tape and the garment seam allowance to ¼" (6mm).
- With raw edges even, place the folded strip on the right side of the garment with 1" (25mm) extending beyond the closing edges. Pin and stitch directionally with grain continuing to the ends of the bias strip.

- Clip the seam allowances, and trim the two extending bias ends to ¼" (6mm).
- Turn the bias strip to the inside, favoring the garment edge slightly so that the binding is inconspicuous. Turn the bias ends in.
- Pin the bias strip in position and slipstitch the folded edge along the seam. Fasten the closing edges with a hook and eye.

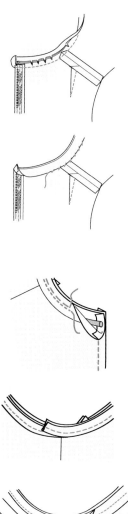

If the facing ends meet, as on an armhole, turn in the ends ¼" (6mm). Trim the excess length and slipstitch free ends together to finish.

cording and piping

This finish can be added to any edge—a neckline, armhole, or hemline—before the facing is applied. The distinction between piping and cording refers to the size of the filler used: piping is thin; cording is thick.

First cut a bias strip the size of the filler plus ¼" to ⅜" (6mm to 10mm) and two ⅝" (15mm) seam allowances. Allow at least ⅝" (15mm) for finishing the ends. Bring the bias strip around the filler, matching the raw edges. With your zipper foot and using 8-10 stitches per inch (3-4 per cm), stitch close to, but not on, the filler. Baste the corded or piped strip to the right side of the garment, matching seamlines. Apply a facing over all piping or cording with a piping or zipper foot. Finish ends of cording following pattern directions.

On an edge without a closing, place the joining at an inconspicuous location.

For narrow piping, pull the bias back, removing a few stitches from the bias so you can cut the filler off where the ends cross. Overlap the two empty bias ends, easing the ends of the bias slightly toward the seam.

For thick cording, do not enclose the filler with bias until you have stitched one edge of the bias to the garment and pieced it. Then, using the proper length of filler for the edge, enclose it in the bias, using a piping or zipper foot. Apply a facing over all piping or cording with a piping or zipper foot.

binding

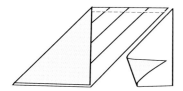

The versatile bias binding was designed to enclose raw edges, thus providing a finish that both conceals and strengthens. To achieve a perfect binding, cut strips of fabric evenly on the true bias, join them on the grain, and press and shape them before application.

cutting bias strips

The ideal bias strip is cut from one piece of fabric long enough to fit the desired area. However, this is not always the most economical usage of the fabric, so piecing becomes a necessity. This can be done in one of two ways-by continuous pieced strips or by individual pieced strips.

For either method, take a rectangular piece of fabric cut on the straight grain.

Fold it diagonally at one end to find the true bias.

Using the bias fold as a guide, mark fabric with parallel lines the desired width of the bias strips, marking as many strips as needed, allowing for ¼" (6mm) seams. Cut away the triangular ends. Mark a ¼" (6mm) seamline on both ends.

METHOD 1

Continuous pieced strips are easy to make.

On the marked piece of fabric, join the shorter ends, right sides together, with one strip width extending beyond the edge at each side. Stitch in a ¼" (6mm) seam and press it open. Begin cutting on the marked line at one end and continue in circular fashion.

METHOD 2

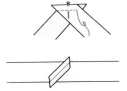

Individually pieced strips are more time consuming.

Cut along the markings for the bias strips. The short ends, previously cut on the grain, will appear diagonal. Mark a seamline ¼" (6mm) from each end. With right sides of the strip together, match the seamlines (not the cut edges), pin, and stitch. Press the seam open.

preshaping the binding

To preshape the strip and to take out the extra slack, the bias should first be pressed, steaming and stretching it gently. You will then have a slightly narrower, taut strip to work with, eliminating the problem of a wobbling seamline. (Note: Commercial binding can be shaped, but the slack has already been removed by the manufacturer.)

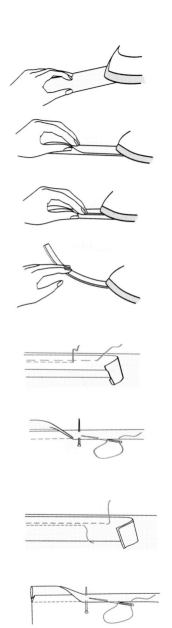

- Fold the strip in half lengthwise, wrong sides together, and press again lightly. For single binding: open, fold cut edges toward the center, and press lightly. A bias binder maker is a helpful notion for pressing single binding

- Shape the tape into curves that correspond to those on the garment by positioning it on your pattern piece and steam pressing. Leave 2" (5cm) extra on the bias strip free at the beginning of any application for finishing.

- Since one folded edge of the finished binding will be even with the seamline of the garment, trim the seam allowance from the edge to be bound.

- When applying the bias strips to the garment, try to place the piecing seamlines at inconspicuous locations wherever possible.

applying the binding

SINGLE BINDING:

Trim the seam allowance from the garment edges to be bound. Cut bias strips four times the desired finished width plus ¼" to ⅜" (6mm to 10mm), depending on your fabric. This will give you ample width for stretching and turning. Preshape your bias strip with a steam iron, as explained earlier, to match the curves of the garment edge. Open out the bias strip and, with right sides together and the raw edge of the strip even with the raw edge of the garment, pin it to the garment. Baste the strip at a distance from the edge slightly less than the width of the finished binding. Stitch next to but not on the basting, so that the basting threads can be easily removed. Turn the bias over the seam allowance. Pin and slipstitch over the seamline.

DOUBLE BINDING or **FRENCH BINDING**: This method makes an attractive finish for sheers.

Trim the garment seam allowances. Cut bias strips six times the desired finished width plus ¼" to ⅜" (6mm to 10mm) to allow for stretching and turning. Fold the strip in half lengthwise with wrong sides together, and press lightly. Preshape the bias to match the garment edge. Trim raw edges so entire strip can be folded equally. Divide it into equal thirds and press again. Open out the folded edge of the strip. With raw edges of strip and garment even, pin the strip to the right side. Baste the strip at a distance from the edge slightly less than the width of the finished binding; stitch next to the basting. Turn the strip over the seam allowances and slip-stitch in place.

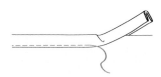

MACHINE-APPLIED BINDING: This is a speedy, one-step method in which success depends upon careful pressing.

Preshape the bias strip as mentioned previously. Instead of folding the tape equally in half lengthwise, fold the bottom half slightly wider than the top half. This overlap on the bottom half will ensure its being caught by the machine stitching. With the wider edge on the wrong side, encase the trimmed garment edge with the folded bias strip. Edgestitch through all layers.

Many machines have bias binder attachments or feet that help guide the pre-folded or flat bias strips while sewing.

special techniques

When bias bindings are used as trim, they often have to be applied around corners, joined together, or ended at a seam or opening.

OUTWARD CORNERS:

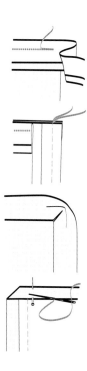

- Open out one prefolded edge of your bias strip; then pin it in place as for single or double binding. Stitch from one end to the corner and backstitch for reinforcement.
- Fold the strip diagonally, as shown, to bring it around the corner. Pin, then stitch the adjoining edge through the corner from one end to the other end. Fold to form a miter at the corner on the right side and turn the bias over the seam.
- To finish the wrong side, form a miter (with the fold of the miter in the opposite direction from the one formed on the right side, so that the bulk of the miter will be evenly distributed).
- Turn, pin, and slipstitch the binding over the seamline, fastening the miter at the corner, if desired.

INWARD CORNERS:

⊷ Reinforce the corner ⅛" (3mm) from your planned seamline, using small stitches. (1)

⊷ Open out one prefolded edge of your bias strip; then pin it to the garment, pulling the corners so the binding remains straight. Stitch from the wrong side of the garment, keeping the binding straight. (2)

⊷ Form a miter on the right side. Pull the fold of the miter to the wrong side through the clip, and form a miter on the wrong side in the reverse direction from the one on the right side. (3)

⊷ Turn, pin, and slipstitch the binding over the seamline, fastening the fold of the miter at the corner, if desired. (4,5)

 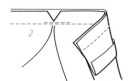

When making machine-applied binding for an outward or inward corner, pin and baste the bias strip to the edge as for single or double binding. Form a miter at the corner, as above. For machine stitching, follow the directions for machine-applied binding, previously described, remembering to pivot at the corners. If desired, fasten the fold of the miter with slipstitches.

JOININGS: When the binding is applied to a long or continuous edge, such as a front closure or hem, a joining is often required. Try to locate the joining in an inconspicuous place.

Apply binding as described in single or double binding. Stop your stitching slightly before reaching the area of the joining.

⊷ Open out the strip and fold the garment so the strip ends are at right angles as they are for piecing. Stitch the ends close to the garment, but without catching the garment in the stitching.

⊷ Trim the seam allowances to ¼" (6mm) and press open. Complete stitching the strip to the garment across the joining.

⊷ Finish by slipstitching the strip to the garment across the joining.

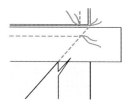

To lap a machine-applied binding, edgestitch to within 2" (5cm) of the starting point, leaving extra binding on both ends. Fold one end to the inside on straight grain, and trim to ¼" (6mm). Trim the other end so it laps under the other end. Pin or baste and continue stitching across the joining. Slipstitch the joining if desired.

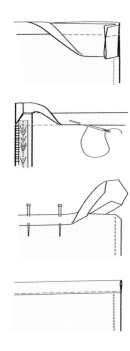

ENDINGS: Binding an edge which ends at a seam or opening requires a special finishing technique. In any of the following cases, the facings should be completed and the seam allowances turned under or the zipper inserted before the binding is applied.

▶ To finish a single or double binding, pin and stitch the binding to the garment through all layers and to the ends of the bias, which extend about 1" (25mm) past the garment opening edge on both ends.

▶ Trim the bias ends to ¼" (6mm) beyond the garment edge. Then trim the garment seam allowance on a diagonal at the corner and fold the extending bias ends back.

▶ Turn the strip over the seam allowance, matching the folded edge with the line of machine stitching. Slipstitch the open ends and the folded edge to the garment.

A machine-applied binding, since it is applied and stitched in one step, requires care in trimming and stitching the ends to achieve a tidy finish.

▶ Fold in about ½ (13mm) at one end on the bias grain and trim, as shown.

▶ To encase the raw edge of the garment with binding, make sure the under edge is deeper than the top edge and that the ends are even. Starting at one end, edgestitch in place through all layers to about 3" (7.5cm) from the other end.

▶ Measure and cut off the binding ½" (13mm) past the garment fold. Trim; fold in the binding end. Complete stitching; finish the open ends with slipstitching.

bandings

Fabric bands can be an important design feature of a garment as well as finish the edge of a neckline, armhole, sleeve, center front opening, or hem.

applied band

An applied band is usually cut from a shaped pattern piece. The two layers are stitched together and then the band is applied to the garment edge.

▶ Staystitch the edge of the garment directionally and insert the zipper, if necessary. Apply the interfacing to one band section. If the band sections have seams, stitch them before you join the band to its facing.

- Pin and baste the band sections together, leaving the notched edge open. Stitch; then trim, grade, and clip the seam allowances. Turn the band and press it flat.

- Pin and baste the outer edge of the one band section to the garment, matching markings at shoulder seams and clipping the garment seam allowance. Stitch from the band side for the best control. Trim and grade the seam, leaving the garment seam allowance the widest. Notch the band seam allowances to eliminate extra fullness so that all seam allowances can be pressed toward the band.

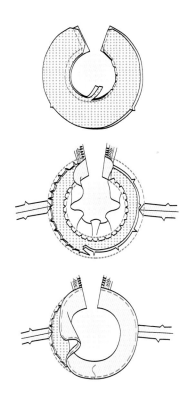

- Turn the band, rolling the seam just slightly to the inside to prevent it from being seen on the finished garment; pin. Turn the remaining free edge under where it falls over the stitching; press and baste close to the edge, if desired. Trim away any excess seam allowance close to the basting.

- Slipstitch the band over the seamline. Fasten the band with hooks and eyes or as instructed on pattern instructions.

When a flat finish is desired for the band, finish the free edge with a stitch-and-overcast, zigzag or serger treatment. Do not turn the edge under, however. Just blindstitch the free edge where it falls, covering the band seam completely. (not shown)

edgestitched band

If a band will be edgestitched, it is often constructed in a slightly different method—the inner band or facing is stitched to the garment and then the outer band is folded over and stitched in place.

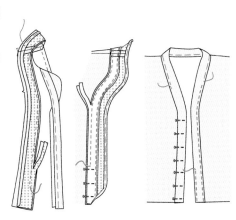

- Interface the band as pattern instructions and stitch any seams in the band sections. Turn in the seam allowance on the notched edge of the band and baste close to the fold. Trim seam allowance to ¼" (6mm) and press.

- Pin the two band sections with right sides together; stitch. Trim and clip the seam allowances. Turn the band and press.

- Pin the right side of the facing band section to the wrong side of the garment, matching markings, and pin. Stitch seam, trim, and press seam toward band.

- On the outside, pin the basted edge of the band over the seam line. Baste to hold band in place for more stability. Edgestitch close to the inner and outer edges of the band.

one-piece placket band

A placket band is a variation of the applied band and is used for an opening extending only part way down a garment.

➤ Apply interfacing sections to the wrong side of the band. Turn in the seam allowances on the sides and lower end of the front band, folding in the fullness at the corners; baste close to the folds. Trim the basted seam allowances to ¼" (6mm) and press. (1)

➤ Pin the right side of the band to the wrong side of the garment front, matching all markings. Stitch along the stitching lines, pivoting at the corners, and reinforcing the corners with small stitches [15-20 stitches per inch (6-8 per cm)] along the seamline. Clip diagonally to the corners and trim the seam allowances (2).

➤ Turn the placket to the right side of the garment. Press long seams toward the band and the triangular end down. Fold the shorter side of the placket along the foldline, placing the basted edge over the seamline, and baste in place. Stitch close to the basted edge, ending at the marking. Baste upper edges together at the neckline. (3)

➤ Fold the other side of the placket along the foldline, and baste in place as above.

➤ Stitch close to the basted edge ending at the marking, being sure to keep the other side of the placket free. Baste upper edges together. (4)

➤ Place lower end of the placket band along the placement line and stitch in place. (5)

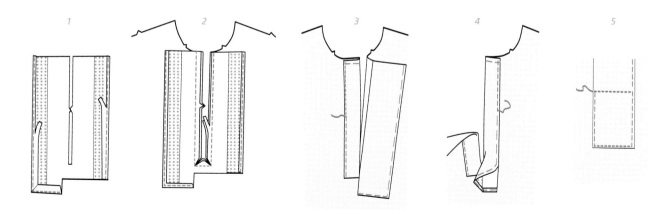

knit bands

Knit bands can be cut from self-fabric or you can use purchased ribbing, which is sold by the yard (meter) or prepackaged. A knit band is always cut a little shorter than the edge to which it is applied. Then the band is stretched slightly as it is stitched to the garment, resulting in a smooth, flat seam.

- With right sides together, seam the band to form a tube, if necessary. Overlock or double stitch the seam and trim close to the second row of stitching. Fold the band in half lengthwise, wrong sides together. (Some purchased ribbings have only one layer of fabric.)

- Divide the band into fourths and mark with pins. (1)

- Pin the band to the right side of the garment, matching the pins with center front, center back and other markings. With band side up, overlock or stitch the band to the garment, stretching the band between the pins, being careful not to stretch the garment edge. If using a straight stitch, stitch again ⅛" (3mm) away from the first row of stitching with either a straight or zigzag stitch, or use an overedge stitch if your machine has one. Trim seam allowances close to the second row of stitching. (2)

- Holding the iron above the seam, steam the band gently to allow it to return to its unstretched state. Press seam allowances toward the garment. (3)

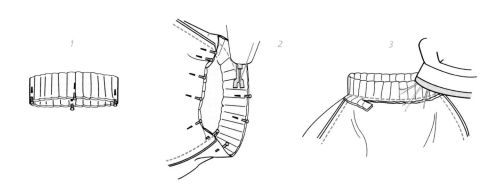

1   2   3

casings

Casings are significant in that they enable fabric to be adjusted into place with elastic or pulled into graceful folds with a drawstring along with providing comfort while adapting to the body shape. One essential principle to be remembered is that a casing must always be wide enough to allow the elastic or drawstring to be pulled comfortably.

SELF-CASING AT FINISHED EDGE:

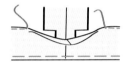

- Mark and then turn in the fabric along the foldline; press. Turn in raw edge ¼" (6mm) and press in place.
- Edgestitch to the garment, leaving the desired opening.
- Self-casings used on a slightly curved edge must be extremely narrow.
- The stitched fold may need to be stretched or gently eased while stitching.

APPLIED CASING AT FINISHED EDGE:

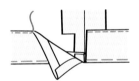

- Cut the casing wide enough for elastic or drawstring plus a ¼" (6mm) seam allowances.
- Right sides together, pin one edge of the strip to the garment, turning ends to inside.
- Stitch in ¼" (6mm) seam; turn to inside, and press.
- Continue as self-casing, leaving the opening at the seam.

WITH A HEADING: The extension for a heading requires extra fabric.

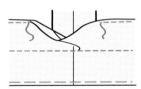

For a self-casing:

- Extend the garment edge, twice the desired width of the heading, plus the casing and a ¼" (6mm) seam allowance.
- Mark heading foldline. Turn fabric to inside and press or baste close to fold.
- Mark casing seamlines. Stitch, leaving desired opening.

For an applied casing:

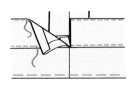

- Extend the garment edge twice the width of the heading plus a ¼" (6 mm) seam allowance. Mark heading foldline. Turn fabric to inside: baste along foldline.
- Cut casing as instructed previously. Turn all edges under ¼" (6 mm) and press.
- From the wrong side, baste casing in place, matching raw edge of casing with raw edge of heading. Edgestitch bottom and top edges of casing to garment, leaving desired opening.

elastic

Using elastic in a casing will ensure regularity in fit. It will breathe and move with you, but will not change from the specific measurement you give it. Elastic is used most commonly in sleeves and waistlines. The opening for its insertion is inside the garment.

▶ Pull elastic through casing with a bodkin or a safety pin, being careful not to twist it.

▶ Lap the ends ½" (13mm) and stitch securely.

▶ Close the opening at the edge of the casing, stretching the elastic as you stitch. For an opening across the casing, slipstitch the opening edges together securely.

drawstring

Cord or tubing knotted at the ends, braid, leather strips, ribbon—anything that captures your fancy can be used as a drawstring. Its length should be equal to the flat measurement of your garment at the casing position plus extra for tying a knot or bow. If your drawstring is too short, you could lose one or both ends inside the casing. The openings for the drawstrings are usually made on the right side of the garment before you make the casing.

There are two types of casing openings for drawstrings.

The eyelet or buttonhole type is made in the outer fabric between the casing placement lines before the casing is applied. Reinforce the opening with fusible interfacing and make buttonholes or eyelets as desired. From the wrong side, stitch casing in place. When the casing is completed, pull drawstring through the casing with a bodkin or safety pin.

The other type of opening is in a seam. Stitch seam, leaving an opening the width of the drawstring, securing each end of the opening by backstitching or lock stitching. Opening can also be secured with bar tacks at each end.

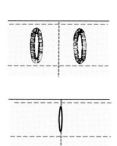

collar basics

A visible mark of quality workmanship on a garment is its collar. Three basic shapes—flat, standing, and rolled—are the starting point for all variations. Here are some guidelines for determining whether or not a collar is well made.

- All collars with corners and center front or back openings should be symmetrical—with identically shaped curves or points.
- The inside edge should smoothly encircle the neck without straining or rippling.
- The underside, or under collar, should never show, nor should seams at the finished edge.
- The collar should hug the garment closely without the corners flipping up or the neck seams showing unintentionally at the back or front of the garment.

Here are some tips to achieve these results.

- Stitch the collar sections together directionally then trim and grade the seam allowances.
- Reinforce corners with tiny stitches [15-20 stitches per inch (6-8 per cm)], trim diagonally, and turn gently.
- To shape the collar, as well as prevent the under collar or outer seam from showing, carefully press.
- Maintain the necessary body and shape of the collar with interfacing, usually cut from your collar pattern.

flat collar

The deeper the curve on the collar neck edge, the flatter your collar will lie. The shape of the neck and the collar are almost identical and has very little roll. The upper and under collar sections are cut from the same pattern piece. The collar itself may be one- or two piece, with or without a front or back opening.

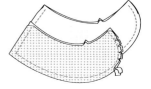

- Apply interfacing to the section that will be your under collar.
- Stitch the collar sections with wrong sides together, leaving the neck edge open.
- Trim, grade, and notch the seams. Turn and press the collar, favoring the outer edge seam of the section that is to be your upper collar.

For either a front or back opening, prepare a buttonhole closure by checking the buttonhole placement; then complete your garment up to the neck finishing. If using a zipper, insert it before or after attaching your collar according to pattern instructions.

- With the interfaced section of the collar next to the garment, pin the collar in place, matching markings, and baste. The upper collar may bubble slightly.
- Finish neck edge with a shaped facing or a bias facing according to pattern directions.

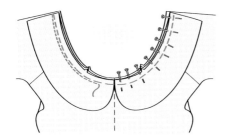

rolled collar

The neck edge of a rolled collar can vary in shape from straight to a curve opposite that of the garment. This collar gently rises from the neck seam and turns down to create a rolled edge around the neck. The line along which the collar is turned is called the roll line or roll. It is usually cut with a one-piece upper collar and a two-piece bias under collar that is slightly smaller.

   This version is suitable for light and medium weight fabrics as the collar is attached to the neckline before the facing is applied. Careful molding and handling of the roll helps to shape the collar.

- Apply interfacing to wrong side of each under collar section. Pick a fusible interfacing that's suitable for shaping or use a sew-in. Stitch center back seam; press open, and trim. For roll collars without a separate under collar, apply fusible interfacing to the under collar side or use sew-in interfacing and long running stitches to sew interfacing to collar at the roll line.
- Stitch collar sections together, stretching the under collar to fit and using small stitches at the points. Trim corners carefully so the points will be sharp when turned. Turn and press the collar, favoring the upper collar at its outer edges so that the seam is on the under collar side.
- Attach garment interfacing and front facing, as necessary. Staystitch the neck edge of the garment and the facing.

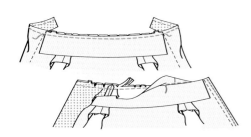

- Baste the collar to the garment, clipping the garment neck edge only where necessary, and stretching or easing the collar to fit as indicated on your pattern. The upper collar may bubble when opened out.
- Staystitch the neck edge of the back facing and join to the front facing.
- Place the completed facing over the collar, matching markings, pin or baste. Clip the facing edge only where necessary.
- Stitch on the garment side. Then trim, grade, and continue clipping the seam through all thicknesses. Turn the facing to the inside; press.
- Understitch the facing according to the pattern instructions.

standing collar

Generally known as the Mandarin or band collar, this basically uncomplicated collar is able to take on many exciting forms. It can be a stiff and close military collar or a soft loose band. This collar will always work and look better if you cut your interfacing on the bias as it will curve around your neck smoothly.—without stiff

- Apply interfacing to collar following pattern directions.

- Fold the collar with right sides together and stitch the ends to within ⅝" (15mm) of the neckline edge. Trim and grade the seam allowances.

- Turn and press the ends only, not the foldline, or you may have an undesirable crease in the finished collar.

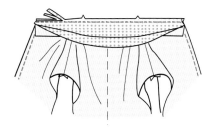

- For either a front or back opening, insert your zipper or facings.

- Baste and stitch the interfaced side of the collar to the garment neck edge, matching all markings and clipping the garment where necessary.

- Trim and grade the seams, leaving the garment seam allowance widest.

- Press the seam toward the collar. Trim and turn in the remaining edge of the collar and slipstitch over the seam. Or follow the pattern directions.

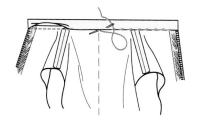

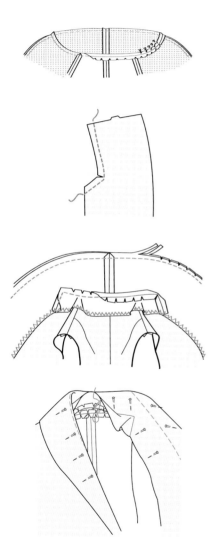

shawl collar

A shawl collar is a special version of the rolled collar in which the upper collar and lapels are cut as one piece. It can vary greatly in shape, having a curved, scalloped, or notched edge.

- Apply interfacing to the garment front and neck edges.
- Stitch the under collar to the garment, stretching the collar to fit and clipping the garment neck edge as necessary.
- Notch the under collar seam allowance to make it lie flat and press the seam open.

Before joining the collar/facing section to the garment:

- Reinforce the inner corner with small stitches along the seamline, pivoting at the marking. Clip to the corner.
- Stitch the center back seam of the collar/facing and press it open. Pin to it the back facing along the neck and shoulder edges, clipping the back neck facing where necessary.
- Stitch, pivoting at corners. Press the seam open. Trim excess fullness at corners.
- Finish the unnotched edge of the facing, if the garment is unlined. Stitch the collar/facing unit to the garment and under collar, stretching the under collar to fit. Trim and grade seams, leaving the garment seam allowance widest; notch curves.
- Turn the collar/facing to the right side and press. Favor the outer edge of the collar so that the seam is on the under collar side.
- Below the place where the collar begins to roll, favor the front edge of the garment so that the seam is on the facing side.
- Try the garment on or put it on a dress form to set the roll of the collar. The roll should be smooth and unbroken and the collar should lie close to the back of the neck. Pin along the roll line.
- When you have achieved the desired effect with the collar/facing in its proper position, pin the facing in place, continue to favor the collar and garment edges as mentioned previously.
- Blindstitch the facing seam allowances, as they fall, to the garment seam allowances at the neck edge. Also blindstitch the facing edges in place.

collar with a stand

Many man-tailored shirts and jackets have collars with stands. Such a collar has practically no roll; it turns down at the top of the stand and nearly always has a front closure.

- ▶ Prepare the collar the same as you would for a **Flat Collar**.

- ▶ Apply the interfacing to the wrong side of one collar stand section. (Sometimes the stand is an extension of the collar, and then the interfacing is applied to both the under collar and stand in one piece.)

- ▶ Pin the interfaced stand to the under collar and the remaining stand to the upper collar, right sides together, and baste. Stitch the ends and upper edge through all thicknesses to within ⅝" (15mm) of the neck edges.

- ▶ Trim, grade, clip, and notch the seam allowances. Turn the stand and press. The collar is now encased in the stand.

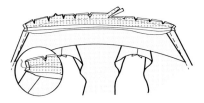

- ▶ Complete the garment front opening according to the pattern directions.

- ▶ Staystitch the garment neck edge.

- ▶ Pin or baste the interfaced stand to the garment neck edge, clipping the garment as necessary. Stitch, trim, and grade the seams, leaving the garment seam allowance widest. Press the seam toward the stand.

- ▶ On the remaining free edge of the stand, trim and turn the seam allowance under and baste close to the fold. Slipstitch the folded edge over the seam. Topstitch if desired. Make machine-worked buttonholes.

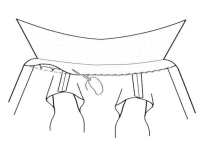

sleeves

A profusion of sleeves is at your disposal, in lengths and shapes to suit every whim. Most of them fall into three basic types.

The first type is the **SET-IN SLEEVE**, which joins the garment in a seam that encircles the arm over the shoulder. The area of the sleeve at the end of the shoulder or upper arm, called the sleeve cap, must be shaped and eased to curve smoothly into the armhole.

The second type, the **RAGLAN SLEEVE**, joins the bodice in a diagonal seam extending to the neckline area, providing a smooth, round silhouette and a great degree of comfort. It tends to be a good choice for hard-to-fit shoulders, since the diagonal seam can be readily adjusted to accommodate differences in the individual figure. Shoulder shaping is achieved by a curved seam or a shaped dart.

The third type, the **KIMONO SLEEVE**, is cut in one with the garment or a part of it, such as a yoke. If it is loose-fitting or short, it may simply be reinforced in the underarm seam, but tighter versions frequently call for gussets or further refinements designed to combine greater comfort with a finer degree of fit.

set-in sleeve

The one-piece set-in sleeve is the most classic and most popular of these sleeves, and allows for many variations in style.

To begin your sleeve, run a line of thread tracing, as shown, along the crosswise grain of the sleeve cap. Easestitch on the right side of the sleeve cap [about 8-10 stitches per inch (3-4 per cm)] just inside the seamline in the seam allowance between markings. An additional row of easestitching ¼" (6mm) from the first row in the seam allowance will give you more control over the fullness and simplify the process of easing.

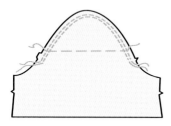

- Pin and stitch the sleeve seam.
- With the garment wrong side out, place sleeve in the armhole, right sides together. Pin together, matching symbols, notches and underarm seam. (1)
- Pull the easing threads up until the sleeve fits the armhole; secure thread ends around a pin in a figure-eight fashion. (2)

» Adjust the fullness and pin about every ½" (13mm). If not indicated by markings, be sure to leave one inch (25mm) of flat area at the shoulder seam where the grain will not permit easing. Baste firmly along the seamline. (3)

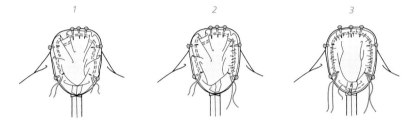

» Remove any pins and try on the garment; adjust if necessary. Tie the ease thread ends securely and remove the sleeve from the armhole.

» Holding the curve of the sleeve cap over a tailor's ham, shrink the fullness by using a steam iron. Begin by steaming the seam allowance to shape the sleeve cap, being careful not to press beyond the stitches.

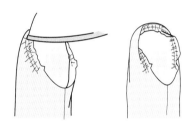

» Hold the sleeve in your hands, and turn in the seam allowance along the ease thread. You should have a smooth rolling sleeve cap without puckers or pulling. If dimples remain on the roll near the seamline, your sleeve may need additional handling when the sleeve is being placed into the armhole for permanent stitching.

» Before you permanently set in the sleeve, complete the sleeve finish. The separate piece will be easier to maneuver than the entire garment. Replace the sleeve in the armhole, pinning and basting it in place. Try it on, checking the shoulder and arm shaping and the sleeve finish.

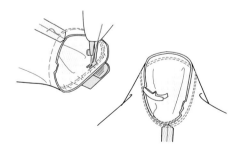

» When the sleeve is set in to your satisfaction, start at the underarm and stitch the armhole seam with the sleeve side up, controlling the fullness as you work.

» Stitch again in the seam allowance ¼" (6mm) from the first row of stitching. To reduce bulk, trim close to this second row.

Never press sleeve cap seam after the sleeve is set in. Simply turn the seam allowances toward the sleeve to give a smooth line to the seam and support to the sleeve cap.

raglan sleeve

This sleeve is well liked for its comfortable fit and relatively easy construction. Its diagonal seamline can lead into another seam or form part of a neckline. It can be cut on the straight or bias grain, with a one- or two-piece construction. The shoulder curve is part of the sleeve shape, and is created by a dart, a seam, or gathers.

- First stitch the dart or shoulder seam and the sleeve seam. Press the seams open.
- Pin and baste the sleeve into the armhole, matching notches, symbols, and underarm seams. Try on the garment.
- The curve of the dart or seam should conform to your own shoulder and upper arm shape, with the sharpest part of the curve neither above nor below the point of your shoulder.
- Test it, standing in a normal position with your arms down. Then swing your arms, making sure there is enough room for comfortable movement. Adjust if necessary.
- Stitch seam, then stitch again ¼" (6mm) away in the underarm seam allowance between the notches. Clip at ends of the second row of stitching, trim close to this stitching, and zigzag or overcast the edge. Press the seam open above the clips.

kimono sleeve

The classic kimono sleeve is a gem of simplicity with its T-shape. However, arms are seldom at right angles to the body; when they are in a relaxed position, the T-shape creates folds. This draped effect can be a graceful design feature in a kimono sleeve with a large opening; however, as the arm opening becomes smaller and shaping adjustments are made to eliminate folds, further sewing refinements are necessary for comfort and strength.

INVISIBLE REINFORCEMENTS

If the sleeve is cut as an extension of the bodice, the main thing to remember is that the underarm area must be adequately reinforced, since it undergoes considerable strain with arm movements.

Method 1

Pin the back to the front at shoulders and sides. Center a piece of stretched bias tape over the seamline at the underarm. Baste both seams, then clip the curve, being careful not to cut the tape. Fit your garment, then stitch the seam, using a smaller stitch [15-20 per inch (6-8 per cm) according to your fabric] on the curves. Press the seam open.

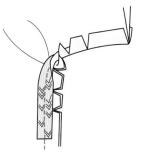

Method 2

Stitch the underarm seam, using smaller stitches on the curve. Clip the curve; press the seam open. Center a piece of stretched bias tape over the open seam and baste through the seamline. Stitch on both sides of the seamline as you spread the clips, catching only the tape and seam allowances.

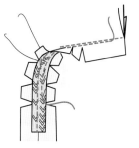

sleeve finishes

A well-made finish enhances the sleeve and handsomely sets off the completed garment.

straight hem

Although it is the most basic and easiest of all sleeve finishes, the straight hem can be quite elegant as it gracefully circles the arm in a smooth curve. After completing your underarm seam:

- Turn up the hem. Baste close to the fold.
- Check to see that the hem is an even depth all around, and trim if necessary.
- Finish the raw edge of your hem with a zigzag, serger finish or overcast.
- Blindstitch the edge to the your garment fabric.

To be sure that your hem will hold its curved line without "breaking", choose an appropriate interfacing. The interfacing you use should be determined by your fabric for the desired effect—whether it be a creased edge or a rolled edge.

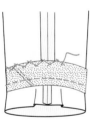

- Cut the interfacing in bias strips equal in length to the circumference of the finished sleeve plus ½" (13mm) and equal in width to the depth of the hem.
- Place the lower edge of interfacing ⅝" (15mm) below the hemline; overlap ends ½" (13mm) and sew.
- Sew the interfacing to the garment or underlining along the hemline with long running stitches and along the upper edge of the interfacing with long catchstitches.
- For a sleeve edge that will be topstitched or edgestitched, trim interfacing along foldline and catchstitch in place.

facings

SHAPED FACING:

▶ Finish the unnotched edge of the sleeve facing as desired.

▶ Stitch the facing ends together. Trim the seam allowances to ¼" (6mm) and press open. Finish raw edge as desired.

▶ Stitch the facing to the sleeve; then trim and grade the seam.

▶ Turn the facing to the inside, favoring the outside of the sleeve, and press.

▶ Blindstitch the free edge to the garment or underlining.

SELF-FACING WITH SLIT: This finish continues part way up the vertical seam and usually includes mitered corners.

▶ Interface the opening and hem before you stitch the sleeve seam. Position the interfacing so that it extends ⅝" (15mm) past the hemline and slit foldlines. Sew the interfacing to the sleeve with long running stitches along the hemline and slit foldlines and with catchstitches along the upper edge.

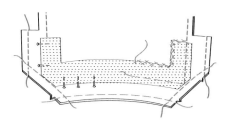

▶ Miter the corners of your sleeve by turning the edges to the outside along the hemline and foldlines; then stitch to the corners. Trim and press the seams open.

▶ Stitch the long sleeve seam to the appropriate marking.

▶ Turn the corners and the facing to the inside along the foldlines and hemline; press. Baste close to the fold. Finish the raw edges, as desired.

▶ Blindstitch the free edges to the sleeve or underlining.

▶ Reinforce the end of the slit with a bar tack on the inside sleeve.

BIAS FACING:

- Cut a 1½" (3.8cm) wide bias strip in a length equal to the circumference of the sleeve plus 2" (5cm).
- With raw edges even, pin the bias strip to the sleeve, right sides together. Pin ends together on straight grain.
- Remove bias strip from sleeve and stitch ends in a diagonal seam; trim to ¼" (6mm) and press open.
- Stitch the bias to the sleeve; trim and grade the seam allowances.
- Turn the bias inside, favoring the right side of the sleeve, and press. Turn the raw edge under ¼" (6mm) and slipstitch.

elastic casings

For a casing at the edge of a sleeve, turn up the fabric along the foldline and baste. Turn in raw edge ¼" (6mm) and edgestitch to sleeve, leaving the desired opening.

Or an applied casing can be formed from a separate strip of fabric or bias tape and applied like a **shaped facing**.

Insert elastic into casing, overlap ends ½" (13mm), and stitch securely. Complete edgestitching. See **Casings** section in this chapter.

For a casing with a heading, which forms a ruffle at the edge of the sleeve, extra fabric is required for the extension. See **Casings** section.

For cuffs that fit snugly around the wrist, a placket must be inserted into the sleeve before the cuff is applied.

LAPPED CLOSING WITH ROLLED HEM: Generally used with a buttoned cuff, this closing allows for a cuff opening without the necessity of making an actual sleeve placket.

- Reinforce the area to be hemmed, using small stitches along the seamline through the markings; clip to the markings. Trim the seam allowance between the clips to ⅜" (10mm).
- Turn in raw edge along stitching to form a rolled hem and slipstitch.
- Whipstitch the ends. Stitch underarm seam, adjust gathers, and apply cuff.

CONTINUOUS BOUND PLACKET: Inserted in a slash, the continuous bound placket can be an extremely durable and simple opening for sleeves. Since the edges of the placket overlap, it can be used with any lapped cuff.

- Reinforce the area to be slashed with small stitches along the stitching line, taking a stitch across the point. Slash to the point.
- Cut a straight strip of self-fabric 1½" (3.8cm) wide and twice the length of the slash. Spread slash open and, with right sides together, place its stitching line ¼" (6mm) from one long edge of strip. Stitch with small stitches on garment beside previous stitching.
- From the right side, press lap away from garment. Turn the free edge in ¼" (6mm) and slipstitch over the seam.
- To keep the lap from turning to the outside, stitch a diagonal line at the top of the fold.
- When a more durable finish is desired, substitute machine stitching for slipstitching.

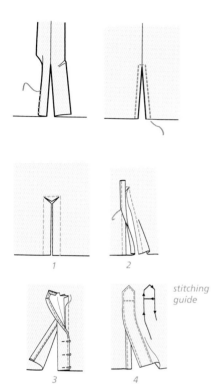

1

2

3   4

stitching
guide

TO MAKE AN IN-SEAM PLACKET:

⚓ Stitch the seam, leaving an opening for the placket at the end of the seam. Backstitch or lockstitch to reinforce opening.

⚓ Press the seam open, leaving the placket seam allowances unpressed.

⚓ Roll the raw edges to the inside; slipstitch in place.

⚓ For a quick and easy finish, turn in raw edges; press. Stitch in place, pivoting across seam.

2-PIECE SHIRT-SLEEVE PLACKET: This sporty finish designed for a man-tailored shirt requires precision and care in its making for a fine professional look.

⚓ Reinforce the sleeve opening by stitching along the seamlines, using small stitches. Slash between the stitches and carefully clip to the corners. (1)

⚓ Stitch the right side of the underlap piece to the wrong side of the back edge of the sleeve (the edge nearer the underarm seam). Trim and press the seam allowances toward the underlap. Turn under the remaining long edge of the underlap ¼" (6mm) and press. Place the pressed edge over the seam allowances and edgestitch through all thicknesses. (2)

⚓ Stitch the right side of the overlap piece to the wrong side of the remaining slashed edge. Trim the seam and press it toward the overlap.

⚓ Stitch the base of the triangular end of the slash to the end of the overlap. Press the stitched end of the overlap up.

⚓ Turn in the overlap at the seam allowances and along the foldlines; press and baste.

⚓ Pin the overlap in place along the folded edges. Keeping the underlap free, stitch the outside fold of the overlap to the top of the opening. Tie thread ends securely on the wrong side. (3)

⚓ Stitching through all layers, stitch across the placket, securing both the point of the slash and the top of the underlap in the stitches; pivot and stitch along the remaining edges of the overlap. Tie ends securely on the wrong side. (4)

The cuff is one design detail that constantly changes, but never goes out of style. Of the two main categories, the primary function of the **EXTENDED CUFF** is to add length to the sleeve, whereas the **TURNBACK CUFF** rolls back to cover the base of the sleeve and often serves solely as a decorative feature.

INTERFACING: The outer layer of the cuff is usually interfaced. Cut interfacing according to the pattern directions.

BUTTONHOLES: Transfer the placement markings to the right side of the cuff with thread tracing before applying interfacing.

extended cuffs

BAND CUFF: This cuff is the simplest of all cuffs to make.

- Stitch the cuff ends together and press open.
- Stitch the gathered sleeve to the interfaced half of the cuff, right sides together. Trim and grade the seam. Press the seam allowances toward the cuff.
- Turn the cuff inside along the foldline, wrong sides together, and baste close to the fold.
- Trim and turn in the raw edge along the seamline; slipstitch it in place over the seam.

It is easier to attach a thickly gathered sleeve to a band cuff before you stitch the sleeve or cuff seams. Attach the gathered edge of the sleeve to the open cuff, matching markings. Trim and press the seam allowances toward the cuff. Then stitch the long underarm sleeve seam and cuff seam at the same time and complete.

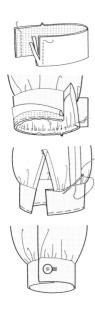

LAPPED CUFF WITH AN OPENING: A buttoned cuff is most often used on full length, gathered or pleated sleeves with a **Continuous Bound Placket** in this chapter.

➤ Apply interfacing to cuff. Fold the cuff lengthwise, and stitch the ends from the fold to within ⅝" (15mm) of the long edge. Trim and grade seams.

➤ Turn and press. Fold under the front lap of the sleeve placket so that the folded edge is even with the cuff edge.

➤ Place the back lap of the sleeve on the cuff at the marking. Stitch the gathered sleeve to the interfaced half of the cuff.

➤ Press, trim, and turn the cuff in the same manner as for a band cuff. Baste close to the fold. Trim and turn in the raw edge of cuff along the seam line. Slipstitch cuff over the seam and extension end.

➤ Complete with button and buttonhole closure.

SHIRT SLEEVE CUFF: A shirt sleeve cuff is used with a shirt sleeve placket and is usually topstitched.

➤ Apply interfacing to cuff as directed. Stitch the cuff sections together, ending ⅝" (15mm) from the long notched edge. Trim, turn, and press.

➤ Stitch the wrong side of the gathered sleeve to the uninterfaced section of the cuff, placing the placket edges even with the cuff edges. Trim and grade the seam.

➤ Press the seam toward the cuff. On the outside, turn in the remaining edge where it falls over the seam and baste in place.

➤ Stitch close to all edges of the cuff and again ¼" (6mm) away from the first line of stitching. Complete with a machine-made or hand-worked buttonhole and button.

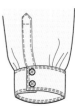

turnback cuffs

Illustrated are two of the most classic examples of straight and shaped cuffs. The variations are unlimited and they can be attached to the sleeve in many ways as well.

STRAIGHT TURNBACK CUFF: Usually a single rectangle cut on the bias or straight grain, a straight cuff can also be two fabric sections. This cuff should be slightly larger in circumference at its foldline than the sleeve to which it is attached so that it can turn back easily.

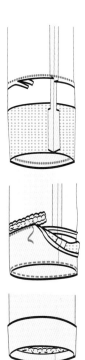

- Apply interfacing to one half of the cuff, extending ⅝" (15mm) beyond foldline and roll line for a softer edge. Stitch the ends of the cuff together. Trim the seam allowances to the foldline as shown and press them open.

- Stitch the uninterfaced side of the cuff to the sleeve, right sides together; trim.

- Press the seam open. Finish raw edge with stitching, lace, (shown) or seam binding.

- Turn the cuff to the inside along the foldline, wrong sides together; baste close to the folded edge. Blindstitch the hem to the sleeve.

- Roll the cuff to the outside over the sleeve. Tack at seam, if desired.

SHAPED TURNBACK CUFF: Made from two fabric pieces, this cuff has many variations.

- Apply interfacing to one cuff piece. Stitch the cuff sections together, leaving the notched edge open; then trim and grade the seam allowances.

- Turn and press the cuff.

- Baste and stitch the cuff to the right side of the sleeve through all thicknesses.

- Finish the raw edges with a **Bias** or **Shaped Facing** in this chapter, stitching through all the layers. Roll the cuff to the outside along the seam, favoring the cuff so the seam is on the inside.

pockets

There are endless variations in pocket types and names. Pockets branch out from two basic constructions—pockets of self-fabric applied to the garment, and pockets of lining pushed to the inside through a seam or slash, and sometimes covered by a flap or a welt.

A few simple but vital rules will bring about successful results:

- Position pockets below the waist so that they are located at a level where your hands can slip into them naturally and comfortably. If placed too near the hem, they will look and feel awkward.
- Pockets above the waist, and patch pockets anywhere, are so often meant to be strictly decorative so you should concentrate on whether their position is flattering, regardless of how accessible the pocket may be.
- If adjusting your pattern, the pockets may require relocating if you shorten or lengthen your garment.

Interfacing for pockets

- All types of pockets made in lightweight or loosely woven fabrics need to be interfaced. Interfacing provides added strength, reinforces the opening, and preserves the pocket shape.
- Welts and flaps should be interfaced if their shape and resiliency are to be preserved.
- Patch pockets usually need no interfacing, but are often lined for a custom finish.
- In-seam pockets will not require interfacing, but may need the reinforcement of a stay to keep the pocket edge from stretching.

patch pockets

Patch pockets are usually made from self-fabric and applied to the outside of the garment. They can be lined or left unlined. When constructing a pair of patch pockets, check carefully to be sure both pockets are the same size and shape and are attached to the garment evenly.

UNLINED:

▶ Turn under the top edge ¼" (6mm) and stitch. Then turn the upper edge of the pocket to the outside along the foldline. Stitch ends and trim. For a rounded pocket, easestitch the rounded area ¼" (6mm) away from the seamline on the seam allowance to ensure a flat finish.

▶ Turn both the hem and the seam allowance to the inside. On a rounded pocket, pull in the easestitches to shape the pocket curve.

▶ If the pocket is square or rectangular, miter all corners. See Chapter 4, Construction Basics, **Mitering.**

▶ Baste around the edges, notching away the excess fullness. Slipstitch the top hem to the pocket.

▶ Complete pocket application following pattern directions.

SELF-LINED: Cut the desired pocket shape twice the length of the pocket plus seam allowances on all sides.

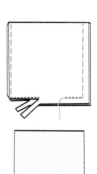

▶ Fold your pocket right sides together and stitch both sides and a portion of the bottom. Leave an opening for turning.

▶ Trim and grade the seam allowances.

▶ Turn the pocket; press it, and slipstitch the opening shut.

▶ Attach to the garment in the same manner as for the unlined pocket.

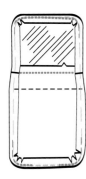

LINED: There are two methods for constructing a lined patch pocket.

Method 1

▶ With right sides together, stitch the pocket lining to the pocket self-facing. Press the seam toward the lining. (For rounded pockets, easestitch the rounded areas on both the pocket and the lining ¼" (6mm) away from the seamline in the seam allowance.)

▶ Turn in the edges of the pocket along the seamlines, drawing up the ease thread where necessary. Starting at the foldline, taper the seam allowances of the lining ⅛" (3mm) so that the finished lining edge will fall ⅛" (3mm) inside the finished pocket edge. Baste close to the edge.

▶ Turn the lining and self-facing to the inside along the pocket foldline. Slipstitch the lining in place around the inside pocket edge.

▶ Attach to garment following pattern directions.

Method 2

▶ Pin the pocket lining to the pocket self-facing, with right sides together. Stitch seam, leaving a small opening in the center for turning the pocket. Press the seam toward the lining.

▶ To ensure that no lining will show at the edges of the completed pocket, trim ⅛" (3mm) from around the lining edge. Fold pocket along pocket foldline with right sides of fabric together.

▶ Align bottom and side edges; stitch along pocket seamline. Trim and grade the seam allowances. For a square pocket, trim diagonally across the seam allowances at the corners. For a rounded pocket, notch out the excess fabric in the curved areas.

▶ Turn pocket to the right side by pulling it gently through the opening. Press pocket, rolling outer seam slightly to the lining side. Slipstitch opening closed.

▶ Attach to garment following pattern directions.

pocket flaps and welts

Just about any type of pocket can be covered or set off by a flap or welt. Both may also appear by themselves as decorative fakes. The major distinction between a flap and a welt is that a flap hangs downward freely while a welt generally points upward and is securely attached along its sides.

   The example shown is a decorative flap, but the same construction principles apply to any flap or wide welt.

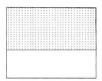

- Interface the outer half of the flap following pattern directions or as desired.
- With right sides together, fold and stitch ends, ending ⅝" (15mm) from the upper edge. Trim and grade the seam; clipping or notching will be necessary for a shaped flap. Turn and press.

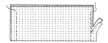

When the direction of the seam allowance coincides with the direction of the finished flap or welt, you must establish the roll of the flap at the seamline so that it will lie flat.

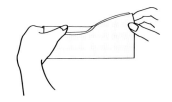

- Turn the seam allowances of the flap down over your hand to establish the roll line, adjusting the flap or welt if more upper fabric is required.
- Pin and baste along the new seamline of the upper portion through both layers. Remember this treatment will be necessary only when the flap or welt turns over its own seam allowance.
- To attach the flap, place the new seamline along the placement lines on your garment and stitch through all thicknesses.

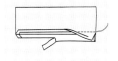

- Turn back the upper seam allowance and trim the lower one close to the stitching.
- Turn in ¼" (6mm) on the long edge of the upper seam allowance, folding the ends in diagonally, and turn it down over the trimmed edge.
- Stitch close to edge. Fold the flap down and press, being careful not to overpress or unsightly ridges from the flap edges will appear on the garment.

- To secure upper sides of corners, slipstitch to the garment from right side, or backstitch heavy fabrics from the wrong side.

welt pockets

A welt pocket gives a very crisp, neat, and precise look to create an essentially tailored appearance. The construction of a welt pocket is similar to a bound buttonhole. It can be made with a single welt, a double welt, or covered with a pocket flap.

Mark precisely and stitch accurately. Use short stitches and begin and end your stitching exactly at the markings. Cut carefully when you are slashing the pocket open. Take time to press after each step and you will be rewarded with a professional-looking welt pocket. If your pocket has a flap, construct and baste in place, following pattern directions.

single welt pocket

For this pocket the welt is pressed upward over the opening of a lining pocket. If your fabric needs more body, interface the welt. Construct and press the welt. It will be easier to work with if you baste the raw edges together on the seamline and trim them to $\frac{1}{4}$" (6mm) from the seamline. Always do any required topstitching before you attach the welt.

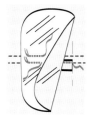

- Pin the welt to the garment, placing the seamline of the welt over the lower stitching line on the right side of the garment; baste.

- Pin and baste the pocket over the welt with the deeper portion above the welt. Stitch along the stitching lines, backstitching or using small knots at the ends.
- Slash between your stitching to within $\frac{1}{2}$" (13mm) of both ends; clip diagonally to the corners.

- Turn the pocket to the inside, turning the welt up. Finish the raw edges of both narrow seam allowances, if desired. Press.
- Position the pocket and garment to carefully stitch around the pocket edges, being very sure to catch the base of the small triangular ends in your sewing.
- Trim and finish the pocket edges, as desired. Slipstitch the ends of the welt in place.

double-welt pocket

This pocket opening looks like a large bound buttonhole. It has two very narrow welts that face each other and is the exception to the rule that welts point upward.

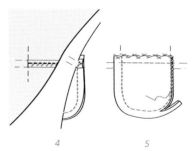

▶ Fold both long edges of the welt, wrong sides together, to meet at the center; press.

▶ With cut edges up, center folded welt over the pocket markings; baste. Slash through center of welt; do not cut the garment. (1)

▶ Baste garment fabric section of pocket in place along upper stitching line over welt, matching markings. Baste lining section in place along lower stitching line in same manner. Stitch through all thicknesses along the indicated lines; backstitch or knot the ends. (2)

▶ From the wrong side, slash through the center for pocket opening. Clip diagonally to ends of stitching, making triangular ends ½" (13mm) deep. Pull pocket parts to inside through slash. (3)

▶ Press welts to meet in center of opening and whipstitch together loosely. Matching pocket edges and starting at the top, stitch side and lower edges together, catching base of the small triangular ends in stitches. (4)

▶ Trim and finish pocket edges. To support weight of pocket, catchstitch upper edge to underlining or interfacing. (5)

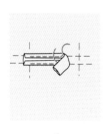

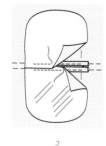

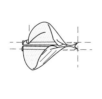

1   2   3   4   5

slanted pockets

Side-front slanted pockets are constructed from two different size pattern pieces—a pocket section and a side front section. The pocket section can be of self-fabric or lining fabric, but the side-front section must be of self-fabric because it becomes a visible part of the main garment at the side seams and the waistline.

If any alterations must be made in the garment pattern pieces, be sure to include the pocket pattern pieces as well.

Because the pocket opening is in a slanted or bias seam, the garment front should be reinforced with a stay to prevent the pocket edge from stretching.

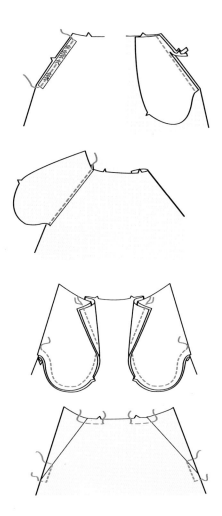

- Cut a piece of ribbon seam binding 2" (5cm) longer than the pocket opening and center over the seamline on the wrong side of the garment front; baste.
- Pin and stitch pocket section to slanted edge of garment front and trim seam to ³⁄₁₆" (5mm), being careful not to cut the seam binding.
- Turn pocket to inside of garment and press. Understitch close to the seamline through pocket and seam allowances to prevent the pocket from rolling to the right side of the garment. Or you can topstitch along the finished edge.
- Pin side front section to pocket section, right sides together, and stitch around the seamline to the side of the garment, keeping the front free. Press and finish raw edges.
- Turn pockets down and baste pockets to the garment front along the upper and side edges.
- Pin and stitch front and back sections of garment together at the sides, catching pocket and side front in the seams; press. Treat the upper edge of the pocket as one with the garment when stitching the waistline seam.

For pockets that have a curved, rather than a slanted seam, the pocket opening should be interfaced for reinforcement. Cut a strip of interfacing 2" (5cm) wide and same shape as the curved seam; baste or fuse to wrong side of garment front along seamline.

inseam pockets

This inconspicuous type of pocket is concealed in side or front seams. The pocket top may be controlled from the inside by a waistline seam. An in-seam pocket is generally made of lining fabric and can be stitched to an extension of the pocket opening or directly to the seamline, depending upon your pattern.

With many fabrics, the seamline on the garment front should be reinforced with a stay to prevent the pocket edge from stretching. Cut a piece of ribbon seam binding 2" (5cm) longer than the pocket opening and baste in place.

Place stay on wrong side of garment front with one edge next to the seamline, as shown. Baste, then stitch by hand or machine ⅛" (3mm) from edge of stay nearest seamline. Stitch one pocket piece to each front and back extension, with right sides of fabric together. Press seams open.

Baste the garment sections together at the seam and across the pocket openings; also baste the pocket edges together. Start stitching from the lower edge and continue around the pocket, pivoting at the corners. Use reinforcement stitches at all pivot points.

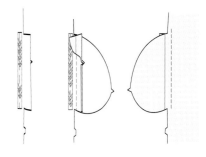

Turn the pocket toward the front along the foldline or roll line. Clip the back seam allowance above and below the facing extension so you can press the seam above and below the pocket. Press lightly for a fold or steam for a soft roll.

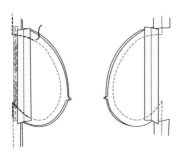

waistlines

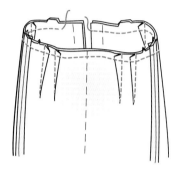

A waistline seam is used to join the top and bottom sections of a garment together and may be straight, curved, or sharply angled.

waistline seams

Usually the skirt section is larger, if only slightly, than the top and must be eased onto the bodice section.

For a fitted skirt:

▸ Slip the bodice inside the skirt with right sides together. Carefully match all seamlines, notches, and markings.

▸ Trim ends of darts and seam allowances diagonally.

▸ Distribute any fullness evenly around the waistline. With bodice side up, stitch along the seamline.

For a gathered skirt:

▸ Pull up the gathering until the skirt is the same width as the bodice. Adjust gathers evenly. (See Chapter 4, Construction Basics, **Gathering**.)

▸ With skirt side up, stitch waistline seam taking care that unwanted tucks or pleats do not form in the gathers.

▸ Press seam toward bodice and finish raw edges, if necessary.

waistline stays

For some fabrics, it may be necessary to apply a waistline stay to prevent the seamline from stretching. The stay is applied after the seam is stitched. Use ribbon seam binding, twill tape, or grosgrain ribbon ½" to 1" (13mm to 25mm) wide.

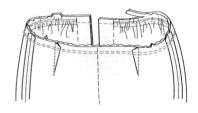

- Cut the stay the exact measurement of the waistline. Length should not include any seam allowance or facings or extensions of any kind.
- Pin and baste to the seam allowances on the skirt side with one edge along the waist seamline and the ends at each seamline.
- Machine-stitch through both seam allowance layers just above the stitched seam. Trim seam allowances to the same width as the stay; do not trim the stay.

For bulkier fabrics, the skirt seam allowance can be trimmed narrower than that of the bodice. For fabrics that ravel, stitch upper edge of stay and seam allowances together.

waistline casings

A casing enables fabric to be easily gathered at the waistline with elastic or drawstring. Use self-fabric (if lightweight), lining fabric, or single-fold bias tape. A waistline casing on a one-piece garment takes the place of a waistline seam. The width of the finished casing must be ¼" (6mm) wider than elastic or drawstring to allow either one to be pulled smoothly through the casing.

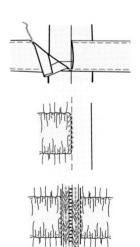

Cut the casing; turn in all edges ¼" (6mm) and press gently. Mark the garment waistline and prepare an opening if drawstring is to be used. (See **Drawstring** section, in this chapter.) From wrong side, place the bottom edge of casing along waistline markings. Stitch along both long edges. Insert elastic or drawstring and finish as required.

If a zipper is used with a waistline casing, end casing at zipper seamline. Insert elastic or drawstring and sew raw ends securely to the casing at each end, keeping garment free.

Insertion of a zipper will secure the ends of the casing and elastic or drawstring. After the zipper is applied, whipstitch seam allowances securely to casing and elastic or drawstring.

waistbands

A properly sewn and fitted waistband is a joy to wear. It never stretches, wrinkles, or folds over as some waistbands have a way of doing, nor does it bind you or slip down on your hips.

To attain this ideal combination of fit, good looks, and comfort, you must know a few general facts about waistbands.

- Most waistbands need the reinforcement and body of interfacing or ribbon seam binding to prevent stretching–particularly loosely woven fabrics and wide or contour waistbands.
- With knits, use elastic in the waistband to ensure the proper stretch and fit.
- Your skirt should be ½" to 1" (13mm to 25mm) bigger at the waistline than the finished waistline measurement of the garment.
- Side closings are on the left side.
- If the ends of the waistband overlap, the overlapping edge faces toward the left or the back. The underneath section usually extends at least 1¼" (3.2 cm) for the underlap.
- Put in the zipper before you apply the waistband, unless directed otherwise by the pattern instructions.

straight waistband

This waistband is cut on the lengthwise grain for the least amount of stretch, and can be constructed in many ways. Base your construction on the type of fabric, the style of the garment, and the wear that it will receive. If using a zipper, position the zipper stop ⅛", (3mm) below the waist seamline. Instructions are for fusible interfacing.

- Cut interfacing for the full width of waistband and fuse to wrong side of fabric or follow pattern directions.
- Turn waistband, right sides together, along foldline. Stitch ends to within ⅝" (15mm) of the edge. Grade seams and trim corner. Turn and press.
- Pin and baste the waistband to the garment, matching markings. Ease the garment to fit the waistband; stitch.
- Trim and grade seams, leaving garment seam allowance widest. Press seam toward waistband.
- Turn in the remaining raw edge and slipstitch over the seam, continuing across the underlap. Fasten with hooks and eyes or desired closure.

If your fabric is fairly heavy or bulky, you may wish to use one of the following methods to eliminate bulk and make a flat, smooth waistband.

Method 1

To reduce the ridge caused when all seam allowances at the waistline are turned in the same direction, lay the waistband pattern piece with seamline of the unnotched edge even with selvage. The selvage acts as a finished edge and is not turned under.

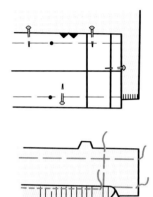

Method 2

This variation produces a thinner, less bulky appearance. Cut the waistband from your fabric equal to its finished width plus two seam allowances. Lap grosgrain ribbon (purchased in the same width as the finished waistband) over the upper seam allowance, even with the seamline; stitch ribbon close to edge.

Method 1 and 2

Finish both waistbands by folding them right sides together along the upper seamline or foldline. Stitch across both ends. Trim corners and grade seam allowances. Turn and press. Attach them to the garment as usual. Slipstitch the selvage of the fabric or the edge of the grosgrain ribbon over the seam, continuing across the underlap. Be sure that the ribbon does not show on the outside.

Method 3

This is a quick, sturdy way to finish a waistband on a casual or sporty garment. Stitch the right side of the waistband to the wrong side of the garment. Press seam toward the waistband. Turn in the remaining edge and baste it over the seam on the right side of the garment. From the right side, stitch close to basted edge through all thicknesses.

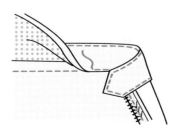

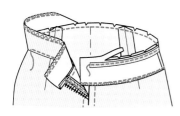

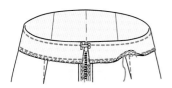

faced waistlines

Skirts or pants without visible waistbands are usually finished with a facing made from lining, lightweight fabric, or ribbon to reduce bulk.

FABRIC:

- Cut and prepare facing.
- Stay the facing waist seamline with ribbon seam binding or twill tape, placing one edge ⅛" (3mm) inside seam allowance; baste.
- Pin the facing to the garment, easing garment to fit.
- Stitch, trim, and grade seams. Understitch facing to keep it from rolling to the outside.
- Turn and press. Turn in ends; sew to zipper tape. Tack facing to garment at seams and darts. Sew a hook and eye at top of closing.

RIBBON:

- Shape a ¾"–1" (20mm–25mm) wide strip of grosgrain ribbon by steaming it into curves corresponding to those of the waistline edge. Shape by stretching the edge that is to be left free; if you shrink the edge to be joined to the garment, it will stretch during wear.
- Fit ribbon to your body, allowing 1" (25mm) for ends.
- Staystitch waistline and trim garment seam allowance to ¼" (6mm).
- Place grosgrain over raw edge of garment with unstretched edge along seamline and ends extending ½" (13mm). Because you are joining two opposing curves, pin or baste carefully, easing the garment to fit.
- Stitch close to edge of ribbon and complete as for a fabric facing above.

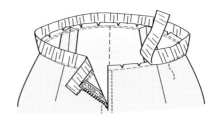

If you are adding a belt and your pattern doesn't include one, you must plan the belt carefully. To find the proper length, encircle your body where the belt will be worn with belting or interfacing in the desired width; add 7" (18cm) to this measurement for finishing your belt. Wider belts extending above your waistline require additional length.

belts

TIE BELT or **SASH:** Your personal preference will determine the type—narrow or wide, bias or straight grain.

- Cut fabric twice the finished width and the desired length (long enough to tie) plus seam allowances.
- Piece where necessary, then fold the sash in half with wrong sides together lengthwise.
- Stitch the ends and the long edge, leaving an opening, as shown. Trim corners and grade seams.
- Turn and press the sash. Slipstitch the opening.

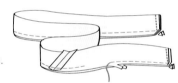

STRAIGHT BELT WITH COMMERCIAL BELTING: Follow manufacturer's directions, or cut one fabric strip on the lengthwise grain the required length and twice the width of the belting plus seam allowances. Shape one end of the belting as desired.

- Fold belt strip right sides together over the belting, and stitch with a zipper foot close to the belting. Do not catch belting in stitches. Trim seam allowances to ¼" (6mm).
- Slide the seam around to the center of belting, and press seam open with the point of your iron. Stitch the shaped end and trim.
- Remove belting and turn; do not press. Slip the belting into the belt, shaped end first, cupping slightly for easier insertion.

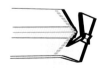

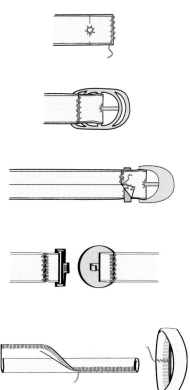

belt fasteners

There are several ways to fasten a belt—with a prong and eyelet buckle, a clasp buckle, hooks and eyes, or snaps. Try on your finished belt. Mark the center front position on both ends for all fastenings but the clasp buckle. Trim the unfinished straight end to measure 2" (5cm) from the center front line. Stitch ¼" (6mm) from the trimmed end and finish as desired.

PRONG AND EYELETS:

- Pierce a hole for the buckle prong at the center front marking nearest the overcast end. Overcast the raw edges of the hole.
- Slip the buckle prong through the hole; turn back the end and sew securely in place.
- For a half buckle, make a fabric belt loop, slide it over belt close to the buckle and secure. Then secure the belt end.
- On the finished end of your belt, make one eyelet at the center front marking and one or more on both sides for adjustments. You may use commercial eyelets, which come in a variety of colors, or make hand-worked eyelets.

CLASP BUCKLE: Slip the ends of the belt through the buckle and bar fastener, folding the ends back along the bars, and try it on. Trim excess at ends to 1" (25mm). Stitch ¼" (6mm) from each end and overcast. Slip the ends through the bars; turn back and attach securely.

FABRIC CARRIERS or **BELT LOOPS:** The loops should be long enough to accommodate the belt width plus ¼" (6mm) (possibly a little extra if your fabric is very thick).

- Cut a straight strip from a selvage edge three times the desired width, and make two folds with the selvage edge on top. Slipstitch the selvage in place.
- Bring ends together and whipstitch. Place the carrier over the markings and sew to the garment at both ends.

THREAD CARRIERS: There are two kinds of thread carriers. One is made of a core of long threads reinforced with blanket stitches, and the other is a thread chain. Fabric carriers or loops are often design features, but thread carriers should be nearly invisible. Use thread that matches your belt. See **Thread Loops** in this chapter.

If you are adding a belt and your pattern doesn't include markings, first establish the belt position on your garment. Make placement marks at desired intervals, and be sure to mark the width of the belt for your carriers.

Although closures are primarily functional, their precision and workmanship can add a special dimension to your garments. From tailored, bound buttonholes to delicate thread loops—from decorative buttons to inconspicuous snaps—there is a wide variety of closures from which to choose.

buttonholes

Let the design and the fabric determine your choice of buttonhole. Couturiers use bound buttonholes for a tailored, professional look on all garments, hand-worked buttonholes for soft or delicate fabrics, and machine-worked buttonholes for man-tailored and casual garments. Your pattern markings include exact placement and size of buttons and buttonholes as recommended by the designer. Any changes from the designer's intended placement or size should be carefully planned.

- If you have adjusted the length of the pattern tissue, adjust the buttonhole placement by evenly spacing them between the top and bottom buttonholes. For bodices, be sure to place a button at the fullest part of the bustline and re-space from there.
- If you are adding buttonholes, the most important consideration in the placement is the size of your button.
- Remember that large buttons are placed farther apart than small ones.
- If your button is larger than recommended, do not move the buttonhole away from the edge, as this will change your center line; rather, extend the closing edge to accommodate the button. (Make this adjustment on the pattern before you cut your fabric so the underlap on the left side will be as wide as the overlap on the right side.)

Always test *the buttonhole on a scrap of your fabric with the appropriate underlining and interfacing to discover any problems you might encounter.*

BUTTONHOLE SIZE: the button should always determine the size of the buttonhole. Minimum buttonhole length is equal to the diameter plus the thickness of the button. Add ⅛" (3mm) to allow for the shank and slight size reduction due to fabric thickness.

   To find the buttonhole length needed for a thick or ball button, wrap a ¼" (6mm) wide strip of paper around the button and mark with a pin where the ends meet. Then fold the paper strip flat and measure between the pin and the fold to determine the correct buttonhole size. Add the ⅛" (3mm) mentioned above.

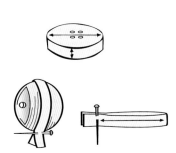

In general, attractive buttonholes are slim, about ¼" (6mm) wide with each lip ⅛" (3mm) wide. They may be slightly narrower for lightweight fabrics and a little wider for bulky fabrics, but total width should not exceed ⅜" (10mm).

PLACEMENT MARKING: Make your buttonhole markings on the right side to make certain that the finished buttonhole will follow the fabric grainlines. First mark the position and length of your buttonhole with pins or chalk, then thread trace for precise markings.

general rules

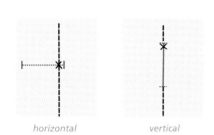

horizontal   vertical

▶ Begin all *horizontal buttonholes* ⅛" (3mm) to either side of the buttonhole placement line—the side nearest the closing edge to allow for the natural tendency of the garment to "pull" away from the closing.

▶ This "pull" is downward for *vertical buttonholes*; begin them ⅛" (3mm) above the actual button placement and directly on the lengthwise placement line.

▶ The reference point in placing your buttonholes is the garment center line; center lines must match when your closing is fastened. This should always be the first line marked.

▶ Next mark the short horizontal lines for the position of the buttonholes and, lastly, the long continuous vertical lines to indicate their length.

▶ The top buttonhole is generally placed below the neckline edge at least half the width of the button plus ¼" (6mm).

▶ The last buttonhole should be 3" to 4" (7.5cm to 10cm) from the bottom, never through the hem.

▶ Buttonholes are not usually placed closer than ⅝" (15mm) from a closing edge; for a large button, the extension should be no less than half the button's width plus ¼" (6mm).

For a **center closing**, the buttons are positioned on the underlap center line, the buttonholes in corresponding positions on the overlap center line.

For a **double-breasted** closing with functional buttonholes, place each row of buttons an equal distance on each side from the underlap center line, and buttonholes in corresponding positions from the overlap center line. Remember the buttons are placed equal distances from the center line, not the buttonholes, and make certain both rows of buttonholes extend in the same direction from the buttons.

For an **asymmetrical closing**, first make sure center lines match. Mark the short placement markings perpendicular to the edge and the long length lines parallel to the edge.

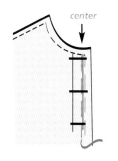

center

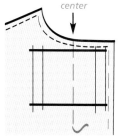

double-breasted

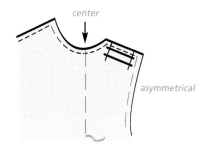

asymmetrical

bound buttonholes

Make bound buttonholes before attaching the facing. They are formed from strips of fabric cut on either straight or bias grain. Those cut on the bias can add an interesting design feature in plaid or striped fabrics. There are several methods for making a bound buttonhole—choose the one that you prefer. There are, however, some techniques that are basic to all the methods.

STITCHING: Carefully stitch, using small stitches [15-20 stitches per inch (6-8 per cm)] and follow the buttonhole markings exactly for precise corners and even buttonhole lips.

TO SLASH OPENING: After stitching, there are two methods of slashing your bound buttonhole. After securing your thread ends, cut through garment at the center of the buttonhole, cutting between stitching lines from the wrong side with small sharp scissors. Slash along the center of the stitching, stopping ¼" (6mm) from each end, and clip diagonally to the ends of the stitching or into the corners, being careful not to cut the stitching. Or, you may cut diagonally through the center of the buttonhole, slashing directly to the ends of the stitching or corners.

SECURING CORNERS: You must carefully secure the ends of your buttonholes if they are not to pull out or ravel when worn. With the garment placed right side up, fold garment back at each end of the buttonhole to reveal the strip ends with the fabric triangle on top. Then stitch back and forth across the base of each triangle several times with small stitches to square the corners and strengthen the ends. Trim ends to ¼" (6mm) and catchstitch them to the underlining or interfacing.

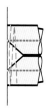

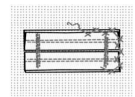

INTERFACING: If you are using lightweight interfacing, make the buttonholes through it so they will be reinforced and supported. Catchstitch ends in place.

TO COMPLETE BOUND BUTTONHOLES: For a quick and easy finish, pin or baste facing to garment through all thicknesses. Hold buttonhole lips together with diagonal basting for hard-to-handle fabrics. Stick a pin from the outside through each end of the buttonhole opening. Be sure that the pins are in line with the grain of the facing. Slash the facing between the pins and turn in the raw edges. Hem around the buttonhole, as shown, taking a few stitches at each end for reinforcement.

To make a better-looking finish on garments to be worn open, establish the length of open buttonhole on the facing with pins. Then cut to within ¼" (6mm) of each end and clip diagonally into the corners.

ORGANZA PATCH METHOD: This method is almost foolproof, and is especially suitable for fabrics that ravel easily or are bulky. Eliminate another problem with these fabrics by applying the interfacing after making buttonholes, rather than making them through all layers. For your patch, always use a crisp, sheer fabric with the same qualities as organza.

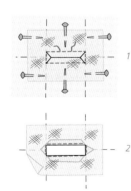

▶ Cut patch 1" (25mm) bigger than the buttonhole. Center the patch over the buttonhole marking on the right side of the garment; pin. If you find the markings difficult to see, emphasize them with tailor's chalk.

▶ Stitch ⅛" (3mm) from each side of marking, using small stitches. Start at middle of the marking, pivot at corners, and carefully count the stitches at ends for accuracy. Overlap stitches where you began. (1)

▶ Slash, being careful not to cut stitching. Turn patch through slash to the wrong side of garment. Press seam allowances away from opening. You now have a neatly finished hole in your garment the exact size of your finished buttonhole. (2)

- Cut two strips of your fashion fabric 1½" (3.8 cm) longer and wider than the buttonhole. Baste the two strips right sides together along the center, forming a seam. (3) Press the basted seam open. (4)

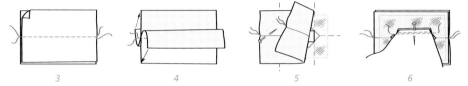

3   4   5   6

- Center the strips on the wrong side of the opening with the basted seam at the center. This forms the two even lips for your buttonhole. Pin the strips in place close to each end. (5)
- Turn the garment to the wrong side. Pin and stitch the long seam allowances to the strips to hold the lips in place, stitching on the garment (outside the buttonhole) alongside the previous stitching so the organza does not show on the outside. Extend the stitching lines ½" (13mm) on both ends of the seam through the organza and strips. (6)
- To cord your buttonhole at this time, **Corded Bound Buttonholes** in this chapter.
- Secure corners, as previously described. Apply interfacing.
- Trim excess fabric from patch and strip, rounding out corners, and press.

ONE-PIECE FOLDED METHOD: This method requires only one fabric strip per buttonhole and is suitable for light and medium weight fabrics.

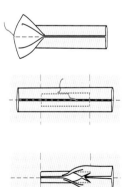

- Cut a strip of self-fabric 1" (25mm) wide and 1" (25mm) longer than the buttonhole. Mark a center line along the length of the strip.
- With wrong sides together, fold edges so they meet at the markings; press. With the cut edges up, baste the center of the strip over the buttonhole markings. Stitch with small stitches ⅛" (3mm) from each side of the center, starting at the middle of the side and going across the ends.
- Carefully count the stitches on the end for accuracy. Overlap stitches where you began. Slash, being careful not to cut through the stitching. Turn strip to the inside and press.
- If you wish to cord your buttonholes, refer to **Corded Bound Buttonholes** in this chapter.
- Fold back the garment and secure the corners as previously described.

TWO-PIECE METHOD: This method is fast and easy for firm fabrics and textured knits.

- Cut a strip of self-fabric 1" (25mm) wide and long enough for all the buttonholes. For the length of this strip, multiply the length of each buttonhole plus 1" (25mm) by twice the number of buttonholes. With wrong sides together, fold strip in half lengthwise and press lightly.

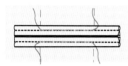

- Machine baste ⅛" (3mm) from folded edge. Strip can be easily corded as you baste; see **Corded Bound Buttonholes** in this chapter.
- Cut the strip into sections the length of the buttonhole plus 1" (25mm) and trim the cut edge to a scant ⅛" (3mm) from the stitching.

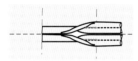

- Baste one strip to the right side, placing the cut edge along the thread-traced position line. Using small stitches, stitch the length of the buttonhole through all thicknesses directly over the stitching on the strip. Leave the thread ends long enough to tie. Repeat for the second strip on the opposite side of the thread-traced line so that the cut edges meet.
- Pull the thread ends through to the wrong side; tie. Slash, being careful not to cut through the strips.
- Turn the strips to the inside and press. Finish the corners as previously described.

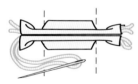

CORDED BOUND BUTTONHOLES: Cording buttonholes reduces their elasticity, but adds body, strength, and durability. Their raised appearance also provides a finer finish. There are two methods for cording bound buttonholes.

For the organza patch and one-piece folded methods, draw a strand or two of string or yarn through lips just before stitching triangular ends.

For the two-piece method, fold strip, wrong sides together, around cable cord or desired filler before you begin to construct the buttonhole. Machine-baste close to the cord using a zipper foot.

machine-sewn buttonholes

There are a variety of styles of machine-sewn buttonholes available today. Traditional square-ended, stretch, keyhole, round-ended and buttonholes for fine fabrics are just some of the variations provided by current sewing machines. Refer to your sewing machine manual for your particular machine for the appropriate buttonhole foot to use for a specific buttonhole style and fabric. Some machines have a different presser foot for sewing automatic buttonholes which helps make a continuous series of same size buttonholes.

Machine-sewn buttonholes are suitable for most garments. Attach any facings or interfacings and apply all markings prior to sewing the buttonholes. Carefully cut the buttonholes open after the stitching is completed.

hand-worked buttonholes

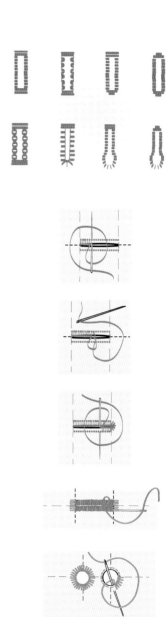

- These buttonholes are sewn through all layers after the facing is applied.
- Machine-stitch a scant ⅛" (3mm) on either side and across both ends of the buttonhole marking. Carefully slash along the length marking.
- Take an 18" (46cm) length of buttonhole twist and insert the needle at one end, anchoring the thread with backstitches on the wrong side.
- Work the buttonhole stitch by inserting the needle through the slash from the right side and bringing it out just outside the stitching line. Keep thread under needle eye and point of needle as shown.
- Draw up the needle so a purl (knot) is formed at the buttonhole edge. Repeat, keeping stitches even and each purl exactly on the edge of the slash.
- Fan stitches at the end closest to the finished edge as shown. Make a bar tack at the remaining end.

BAR TACK: Finish both ends of the buttonhole with a bar tack. First take 3 or 4 long stitches across the width at each end of the buttonhole. Then work the blanket stitch over the core threads, catching the fabric underneath.

EYELET: This type of buttonhole is used with studs, cuff links, drawstrings and belts. Sew around placement marking with small running stitches. Cut an opening the desired size or punch a hole with an awl. Bring needle up through fabric from the wrong side a scant ⅛" (3mm) from edge of hole. Leave 1" (25mm) of thread on the wrong side and work around the hole with buttonhole stitches. Fasten threads securely on the wrong side.

fabric and thread loops

Fabric and thread loops are perfect examples of those little touches that add greatly to the pleasure of wearing a garment you have made. With careful planning and accurate marking they can be easier to make than they look.

fabric loops

Fabric loops can add an impressive touch to a simple style. They can be made of self-filled or corded bias tubing, in contrasting or self-fabric, purchased braid, or other tubular material that complements your garment fabric.

SELF-FILLED TUBING: Cut a bias strip the desired length and the finished width plus enough seam allowance to fill the tubing. The additional seam allowance depends upon your fabric— the bulkier the fabric, the narrower the seam allowances. Experiment to determine the correct width for your particular fabric. Remember also that the strip will become somewhat narrower as it is stretched during stitching.

▶▶ Right sides together, fold bias in half lengthwise and stitch, stretching bias as you sew. At end, slant the stitching diagonally, making the tube wider.

▶▶ To turn, pass a heavy thread and a tapestry needle, eye first, through the bias or use a loop turner or bodkin.

▶▶ For narrow tubing, turn in the raw edges, roll bias between your fingers, and sew edges together, eliminating turning process. (not shown)

CORDED TUBING: Cut a bias strip of fabric the desired length and wide enough to fit around the cord plus ½" (13mm) for seam allowances and stretching. If necessary, piece the bias. Cut a piece of cable cord twice the length of the bias; the extra cord will facilitate stitching and turning.

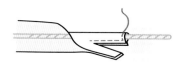

▶▶ Fold the bias over the cord with right sides together and edges even. Place one end of the bias ¼" (6mm) beyond the center of the cording.

▶▶ Using a zipper foot, stitch across the end at the center of the cording. Then stretch the bias slightly while stitching the long edge close to the cording. Trim the seam allowance.

▶▶ To turn right side out, slowly draw the enclosed cord out of the tubing; the free cord will be pulled into the tubing automatically. Cut off the stitched end and the excess cording.

ATTACHING LOOPS: Fabric loops can be applied singly or in a continuous row, depending on the fabric weight and spacing desired. Mark the seamline the length of the closure area on a strip of lightweight paper. Make a line for the distance that the loops are to extend (approximately half the diameter of the button, plus the thickness of the cording). Make spread of each loop equal to button diameter plus twice the cord thickness.

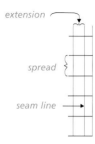

extension

spread

seam line

Single loops: Cut each loop the correct length to fit within the markings plus two seam allowances. Form each loop with the seamed side up and the loop pointing away from the edge, keeping the edges of the paper guide and the loops even. Use narrow masking tape to hold them in place. Using large stitches, stitch on the paper close to the seamline within the seam allowance. Then remove the masking tape, pin paper guide to the appropriate garment edge on the right side of the fabric, matching seamlines. Stitch close to seamline near first stitching. Tear away paper and apply facing.

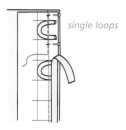

single loops

Continuous loops: With a long strip of bias tubing, form a continuous row of loops on the paper guide within the markings, extending them ½" (13mm) into the seam allowance. Tape and stitch them to the paper and then apply them to the garment in the same manner as single loops. Cut the short looped ends in the seam allowance so loops lie flat. Ends may be trimmed to ¼" (6mm) to reduce any unnecessary bulk before applying facing.

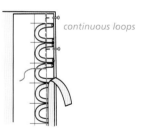

continuous loops

thread loops

A blanket stitch or a thread chain can form all types of loops. A thread loop is usually placed at the corner of a neck opening and fastens to a small button. It is also often used in place of a metal eye on delicate fabrics or in conspicuous locations. Its length should be equal to the diameter plus the thickness of the button. A longer loop is used to form a belt carrier. Usually placed at the side seams, it should be just large enough to let the belt slip through.

BLANKET STITCH: The blanket stitch is the classic stitch used for most thread loops. Use matching double thread or single buttonhole twist.

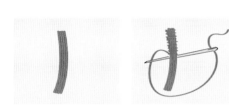

▸ Take 2 or 3 foundation stitches the desired length and depth of your loop, securing the ends with small backstitches. These stitches form the core of your loop, and it is essential that they be the correct size.

▸ With the same thread, work blanket stitches closely over the entire length of the foundation threads.

THREAD CHAIN: If you prefer, a thread loop can be made with the chainstitch.

▸ Use a double thread or single strand of buttonhole twist securely fastened to the garment with one or two small overlapping stitches.

▸ Form a loop on the right side by taking another short stitch. Slip the thumb and first two fingers of your left hand through the loop while holding the needle and thread end in your right hand.

▸ Using the second finger of your left hand, pick up a new loop and pull it through the first loop, tightening as you proceed.

▸ Continue to work the chain to the desired length. Place the needle through the last loop to form a knot and end the chain. Secure the free end with several small stitches.

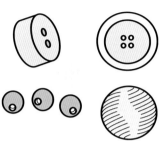

Buttons are an important finishing touch not only in their more practical sense as fasteners, but also as adornments and essential parts of the garment design.

BUTTON PLACEMENT: The time it takes to see that your buttons are placed correctly is well spent, for it ensures that your garment will close in a straight line and lie flat. Pin the garment closed, matching center basting lines.

For a **horizontal buttonhole**, push a pin through the end of the buttonhole near the finished edge of the garment. The center of the button should be sewn at this point and directly on the center front or center back line.

Vertical buttonholes have the buttons placed ⅛" (3mm) below the top of the buttonhole and on the center front or center back line. Place each button directly in line with the previous button.

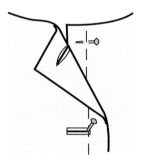

horizontal buttonholes

vertical buttonholes

THREAD: To sew on the button, use a double strand of polyester or cotton thread, heavy-duty thread, or buttonhole twist. For buttons on heavier weight coats and jackets, button and carpet thread may be used. Drawing your thread through beeswax will prevent knots from forming in the thread while you sew. For easy handling, your thread should not be much longer than 18" (46cm). Secure your thread with a couple of small backstitches on the right side under the button, rather than with a knot, for a neater application.

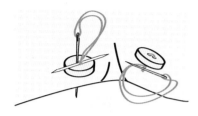

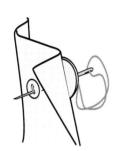

SEW-THROUGH BUTTONS: These should have a thread shank to allow the buttoned fabric to lie smoothly and not pull around the buttons. The length of the shank should equal the thickness of the garment at the buttonhole plus ⅛" (3mm) for movement. Always begin sewing on the right side. Place a pin, matchstick, toothpick, or other object over the button and sew over the object when sewing on the button. Remove the object, raise the button to the top of the stitches, and wind the thread tightly under the button to form the thread shank. Backstitch several times into the shank for a secure finish. Buttons used for trim will not need a shank. Many sewing machines have a special presser foot and built-in button sew-on stitch.

REINFORCED BUTTONS: For coats and suits, reinforced buttons are advisable. Place a small flat button on the back of the garment under the larger button. Sew directly through from one to the other for added stability. Use a small folded square of ribbon seam binding in place of the reinforcement button for delicate fabrics. Place it inside the garment directly beneath the holes where it cannot be seen when worn.

SHANK BUTTONS: Attach the button with small stitches sewn through the shank. The direction of the shank should always be aligned with that of the buttonhole. (not shown)

Zippers can be made of metal or synthetic teeth or coils and are available in a variety of sizes and wide range of colors to coordinate with your fabric. Specialty zippers, such as separating, invisible, and heavy-duty versions, can also be purchased. If you can't find the zipper you need, you can have one custom-made!

basic application procedures

The length of the zipper and the specific type required, if any, will be indicated on the back of your pattern envelope. When you make your zipper selection, consider the weight of the zipper in relation to the weight of your fabric. You will find that zippers won't be the least bit tricky if you follow the directions carefully and rely on these basic application tips:

- Close the zipper and press out creases before application.
- Always close the zipper before laundering or dry cleaning.
- Staystitch the zipper opening edges directionally in the seam allowance.
- Always pin the zipper from the top downward, unless otherwise indicated.
- Bias seams or stretchy fabric may require a stay before inserting the zipper. Cut two strips of seam binding the length of the opening, and baste to the wrong side along the seamline in the seam allowance.
- Extend seam allowances of the zipper opening with ribbon seam binding if they are less than $\frac{5}{8}$" (15mm) wide.
- For zippers with cotton tape, preshrink the zipper if it will be applied in a washable garment.
- Remember that plaids or stripes should match at the zipper closing as well as at other seams; baste the closing shut, matching the pattern of the fabric.
- A zipper foot is essential for machine stitching and, if it is adjustable, permits stitching on either side of the zipper without turning the fabric. Always sew both sides of your zipper in the same direction.
- When pressing the zipper area on the right side of the garment, use a press cloth to prevent any unsightly shine, puckers, or impressions.

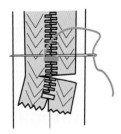

SHORTENING A ZIPPER: Zippers can be shortened from either end though many prefer to shorten the zipper from the top. Make sure the zipper ends are sewn into a seam.

To shorten from the top, place the zipper stop slightly above the bottom of the opening. Stitch the zipper and apply the waistband or facing before trimming the excess zipper tape from the top, otherwise there is nothing to prevent the slider from coming off. Separating zippers should be shortened only from the top. (not shown)

To shorten from the bottom, measure the desired length and whipstitch or bartack by machine across the teeth or coil to form a new bottom stop. Cut the zipper ½" (13mm) below the stitching. Apply the zipper as usual.

STITCHING A ZIPPER: For an attractive appearance, the final stitching that shows on the outside of the garment must be straight and an even distance from the zipper opening.

- For best results, topstitch from the right side of the garment using thread basting or sewing tape as a guide.
- Always begin your stitching at the bottom of the zipper placket and stitch to the top.
- To stitch past the slider, pull the tab up and turn the slider on its side, or leave the needle in the fabric, raise the zipper foot, and move the slider down before completing your stitching.

One of the easiest methods of achieving straight, even stitching is to use a tiny prickstitch and complete the final stitching by hand. This method is a custom technique and is especially desirable on delicate and pile fabrics.

centered application

This application is the one most frequently used for center front, center back and sleeve openings. Attach the facing before or after installing the zipper. Example is shown with facing attached before zipper installation. Complete facing construction according to the pattern instructions or as shown.

- Open out facings. Machine-baste opening edges together along seamlines, and press seam open.
- Face down, place closed zipper on opened seam allowances with zipper teeth centered over the seamline and the pull tab ¼" (6mm) below neck or waist seamline; baste.

- On outside, stitch by machine or hand across lower end and continue along one side, ¼" (6mm) from basted seam.
- Begin again at lower end and stitch other side in same manner.
- Turn the facings to the inside, folding in the ends to clear the zipper teeth. Slipstitch the ends in place. Anchor the remaining facing edge. Fasten the neck edge with a hook and eye on the inside of your garment.

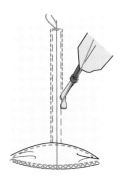

lapped application

This method neatly conceals your zipper, making it particularly suited for zippers that do not match perfectly with the color of your fabric. It is also used for openings in the side seams of garments. When the garment edge is faced, the facing may be attached before the zipper is inserted.

- Mark the seamline on the underlapped opening edge with thread tracing. Turn in the edge ⅛" (3mm) from the traced seamline in the seam allowance; baste and press. A tiny fold will appear in the seam allowance at the lower edge.
- Turn in the full seam allowance on the other opening edge; baste and press.
- Place the underlapped edge over the zipper tape with the bottom stop of the zipper even with the end of the garment opening. Baste close to the zipper teeth, leaving enough room for the tab to slide easily. Stitch close to the edge by hand or machine.
- Position the overlapping edge to just cover the stitching on the opposite side of the opening. Baste the remaining zipper tape in place to be sure it does not shift during stitching.
- Stitch by machine or hand across the lower end, pivoting at the corner and continuing along the side ⅜" (10mm) from the edge.

Continue following pattern directions.

mock fly-front placket

This version is the simplified method usually found in women's patterns. Remember that the placket in women's garments always laps right over left, just the opposite of men's.

- ▸ Turn in both front extensions along the foldlines and baste close to the folds.
- ▸ Pin or baste the closed zipper under the left front, with the teeth close to the basted edge and the pull-tab ⅛" (3mm) below the waist seamline. Stitch close to the edge.
- ▸ Lap the right front over the zipper, even with the center front marking on the left front, and baste close to the fold through all thicknesses.
- ▸ On the inside, baste remaining zipper tape to the right front, through all thicknesses.
- ▸ On the outside, stitch on the right front along the stitching line, ending at the seamline marking. Pull threads to the inside and tie.

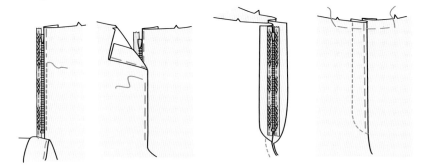

special applications

DRESS SIDE PLACKET: For a placket located on the side of a dress, the zipper is inserted in a seam that is closed at both ends. To make a top stop for the zipper, simply whipstitch the upper edges of the zipper tape together. Before inserting zipper, be sure the opening length is equal to the zipper length, with the bottom stop barely concealed. If the zipper is too long, shorten it as previously described in this section. Insert your zipper, using the lapped or centered application, ignoring facing instructions. As you complete the zipper, stitch across the bottom end, along the long edge, and across the top end by machine or by hand.

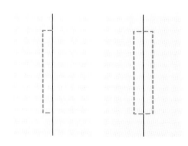

INVISIBLE ZIPPER: The invisible zipper, which has no rows of stitching on the outside of the garment, is easily stitched with a special invisible zipper foot or a regular zipper foot. Unlike other zippers, the invisible zipper is applied to the opening edges before the remainder of the seam is stitched. The facings are usually applied after the zipper is installed.

- Open the zipper and place it face down on the right side of the fabric. Have the teeth lying on the seamline and the tape in the seam allowance.
- Lower the right-hand groove of the foot over the teeth, and stitch from upper edge to pull tab. Keep stitches as close to the teeth as possible.
- Close the zipper to position the other side on the opposite seam allowance. Pin or baste as desired.
- Open the zipper and stitch with the left hand groove of the foot over the teeth.
- Close the zipper. To finish the seam below the zipper, slide the zipper foot to the left. Lower the needle and begin stitching just slightly above and to the left of the last stitch. Stitch seam closed.
- To complete the application, stitch each end of the zipper tape to the seam allowances.

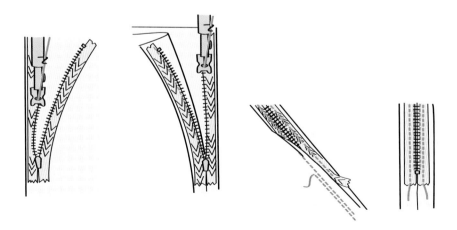

fasteners

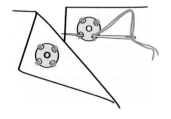

There are many commercial fasteners available. These fasteners should be chosen in a size appropriate to the fabric weight, the amount of strain the closure will receive, and the type of cleaning and care the garment will require. They should be inconspicuous while the garment is being worn.

snaps

These fasteners are used on overlapping edges that receive a minimum of strain. The ball half of the snap is sewn on the underside of the overlap. The socket is sewn on the upper side of the garment section closest to your body.

- Sew the ball on first. Take several small stitches close together through each hole, picking up a thread of the garment with each stitch. Carry the thread under the snap from hole to hole.
- To mark the location for the socket, rub tailor's chalk onto the ball and position the garment as when fastened, or use a pin through the ball section.

hooks and eyes

Hooks and eyes are most frequently found at neck edges or waistbands.

- To attach the hook, work stitches around the circular holes, picking up a garment thread with each stitch. Secure the thread, but do not clip. Slip the needle through the fabric, surfacing to sew the hook end to the garment to hold it flat.
- To fasten straight or curved metal eyes, work stitches around the circular holes as for the hook.
- For curved metal eyes, continue to sew a few stitches on either side of the eye to hold it flat. Or, use a thread loop.

If the edges overlap, sew the hook even with the overlapping edge on the inside. Then sew a straight metal or thread eye on the outside of your garment on the underlap.

If the closing edges just meet, such as a neckline, sew a hook and a curved metal eye on the wrong side of the garment.

- Place and sew the hook $\frac{1}{16}$" (2mm) from one edge. The curved eye should be placed with the loop extending slightly beyond the other edge.
- Or make a thread eye, the same length as the metal eye it replaces.

Large or heavy-duty hooks and eyes are used on areas that receive excessive strain. Position them as you would regular hooks and eyes and sew them on through the holes.

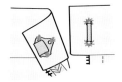

hook and loop tape fasteners

This fastener has tiny hooks on one side , the other has a pile fabric serving as minute eyes. When pressed together, the two strips fuse until pulled apart. The fasteners are not suitable on tight-fitting garments, on very lightweight fabrics, or whenever extra bulk is not desirable. There are several effective methods of application.

- Machine-stitch the lower strip in place through all layers and the upper strip through just one layer where it cannot be seen. This application must be done during the construction process.
- Another method is to apply the upper strip by hand, using a sturdy slipstitch through just one layer of fabric, and the lower strip by machine through all layers.
- Topstitching both strips through all garment layers is also popular as a design detail on casual clothes.

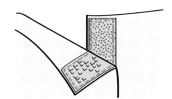

hems

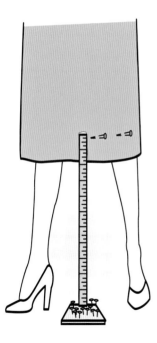

One of the most important fashion aspects of any garment is its hemline. Although the real purpose of the hem is to help your garment hang well by adding weight to the edge, variations in hem lengths will also change the silhouette and proportion of your garment. To be really complete, your wardrobe should include several different hemline heights.

There is no standard hem length that is correct for every woman. Always let the lengths most becoming to you influence your choice of hem levels.

MARKING HEMLINE: When preparing a hem, there are several fundamental steps to follow. As with any other phase of fitting, the proper undergarments and shoes must be worn when measuring the hem. If you plan to add accessories such as a belt, sash, or jacket, wear it while you are measuring. It will be a factor in determining the hem length in proportion to the total garment design and will affect the garment length considerably when worn.

- For absolute accuracy, always have someone mark your hem for you. To avoid discrepancies, stand stationary and have the person doing the marking move around you,
- Pins should be placed every 3" (7.5cm) for a straight skirt and every 2" (5cm) for a flared skirt.
- If your garment has a bias cut or circular hem, let it hang for 24 hours before measuring, allowing the bias to set. Then mark the hem. This prevents hemline sag.
- After the hemline has been marked, pin up the hem to see if it looks good. Insert the pins at right angles to the hemline, letting it fall in a natural manner.
- Regardless of length, the hem should look right. It should be parallel to the floor, but occasionally a perfectly straight hem will appear uneven, especially in garments with pleats, plaids, or that are bias cut. If such a situation occurs, the hem must be changed to adapt to the optical illusion. Make the correction, using a carefully controlled, gradual change in the hem depth; then try the garment on again to see if the hemline appears to be even.

types of hems

PLAIN HEM: This hem, the simplest and most basic of all the hems, has little or no fullness. The procedures used to complete it are the preliminary steps for most hems.

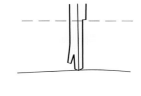
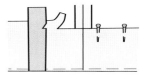

- Trim any seam allowances below the hemline to ¼" (6mm), eliminating bulk that could cause ridges when the hem is pressed.
- Baste close to the fold of the hem, measure the hem depth, and trim evenly.
- Press the hem with brown paper between the hem and the garment, steaming out any fullness.
- Finish the raw edge in the manner best suited to the style and fabric. Sew the hem in place with a slipstitch or hemming stitch for turned-under or seam binding finishes and blindstitch for pinked or overcast finishes.
- Use the pressing techniques applicable to the hem edge desired. See **Pressing** in this chapter.

EASED HEM: When your hem has excess fullness that must be adjusted, an eased hem should be used. To ease, stitch ¼" (6mm) from the raw edge, using long stitches. Pull up the ease thread every few inches (centimeters), then shrink out the fullness with a steam iron. Refer to **Pressing** in this chapter, for detailed information on how to shrink hems. Finish the raw edge and sew as suggested for the plain hem.

CIRCULAR HEM: This hem should be about 1" (25mm) in depth to eliminate bulk and excess fullness. Let the garment hang for 24 hours before marking. Then mark and complete hem, following the steps for the eased hem.

NARROW HEM: For blouses, lingerie, and accessories, use a narrow hem. Trim hem allowance to ½" (13mm). Turn under raw edges ¼" (6mm) and press. Turn up edge again and press. Stitch by machine through all thicknesses for casual clothes, or slipstitch to complete the hem.

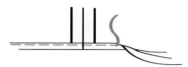

MACHINE-STITCHED HEM: A machine-stitched hem is suitable for garments in which stitching has been used elsewhere as a decorative element. Fold hemline to desired width. For woven fabrics, turn under hem edge ⅜" (10mm) and press. From right side of fabric, stitch close to upper edge. If desired, a second row of stitching can be placed ¼" (6 mm) below the first row.

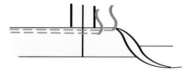

COVER STITCH HEMS: There are two types of hem finishes for knit fabrics sewn on the overlock machine besides a traditional serger blindhem. Using two or three needles, the cover stitch hem resembles topstitching on the right side.

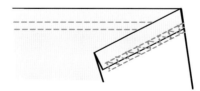 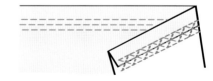

hem finishes

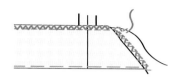

STITCH AND MACHINE ZIGZAG: Stitch ¼" (6mm) from raw edge, using a large stitch if your hem will be eased. Machine zigzag edge, using this stitching as a guide. To ensure an invisible hem, turn the edge back ¼" (6mm) and blindstitch.

STITCH AND PINK: Stitch ¼" (6mm) from the raw edge; use a large stitch for an eased hem, then pink or scallop the edge. Turn edge back ¼" (6mm) and blindstitch to garment.

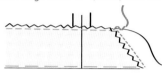

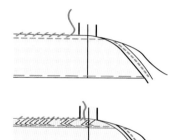

TURN-UNDER: Use this finish for light and medium weight fabrics, for sheers, and for limp hems. Turn in the raw edge ¼" (6mm) and stitch close to the fold. Use hemming stitch to complete hem.

SEAM BINDING or BIAS TAPE: Use for loosely woven fabrics that tend to ravel. Stitch tape or seam binding ¼" (6mm) from the raw edge of the fabric. For bias tape, easestitch the hem, adjust fullness, and machine stitch the tape to the raw edge. Complete the hem using hemming stitch. For bulky fabrics, fold back tape and blindstitch fabric edge to garment.

OVEREDGE: This overlock stitch is a good edge finish for fine fabrics as it is not bulky.

special hems

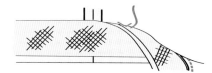

BIAS-FACED HEM: A facing constructed of a lightweight fabric will provide a smooth finish for garments with inadequate hem allowances, very full skirts, or very bulky fabrics. You may use either a commercial bias facing or your own bias strip cut from a lightweight material the desired width plus ½" (13mm) for seam allowances.

Mark your hemline, leaving at least ½" (13mm) additional fabric at the bottom edge. For a very curved hemline, shape the bias to the garment. Match raw edges and stitch in a ¼" (6mm) seam. Join the ends of the facing following instructions under Binding, **Joinings**, in this chapter. Press seam open. Turn in raw edge ¼" (6mm), turn facing up, and slipstitch.

HEMS WITH PLEATS: Press open the seam within the hem area where it crosses the hem at the edge of a pleat fold. Finish the raw edge of the hem, then measure up from the hemline the width of the hem and clip the seam. Both seam allowances above the hem will face in one direction, helping to keep the pleat fold flat.

After hemming, an effective way to ensure that any pleated hem stays creased is to edgestitch the fold of the pleat. Stitch through all thicknesses of the hem on the inside.

To handle fullness effectively in a pleated hem, re-stitch the seam below the hemline at a slant opposite that of the garment seam above the hemline. Remove previous stitching and trim the seam below the hemline to ¼" (6mm). Complete the hem.

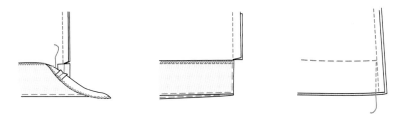

That finely finished look every woman strives for is as much a product of good pressing as it is of careful construction. Do not ignore pressing directions in your haste and zeal. If you postpone your pressing until the garment is completed, it will be too late to accomplish well-defined edges and sculptured contours. Set up your pressing equipment near your sewing machine and use it faithfully.

The most important idea to remember is that pressing is not ironing. Pressing is the process of lifting the iron and setting it down in the proper position. You can use pressing to accomplish feats not possible with a needle and thread.

Specifically, pressing techniques depend on the particular fabric and garment construction, but there are some basic rules which should always be followed:

- Have an assortment of equipment available so that you can place the fabric in the most practical position for the area being pressed.

- Always test an odd scrap or an inconspicuous area to determine the best technique for your fabric. Test a piece large enough to allow a comparison between the pressed portion and the unpressed portion. Check your fabric's reaction to steam and moisture. Both should be used sparingly, or water marks, puckering, and dulling may result.

- Press with the grain of your fabric whenever possible; be very careful not to stretch edges or curves by pulling the fabric.

- Whenever possible, press on the wrong side of your fabric. If you must press on the right side, use a press cloth.

- Use brown paper strips to prevent impressions of seam allowances, darts, or pleats from appearing on the right side of your fabric. Cut strips at least 2" (5 cm) wider than the area to be pressed.

- Always press seams and darts before they are crossed with other seams to eliminate any extra bulk.

- Never press any sharp creases until the fit of your garment has been double-checked. Try to use only the tip of your iron and work in the same direction as you stitched. To avoid marring fabric, do not press over basting threads or pins.

- Above all, know your fabric, and do not over-press.

PRESS CLOTH: To prevent shine and protect your fabric from the heat of the iron and its impression, use an appropriate press cloth between the fabric and the iron. Press cloths are made of a variety of fabrics. The one you use depends upon the nature of your garment fabric. When in doubt which press cloth is best for your fabric, use a scrap of self-fabric.

STEAM: The moisture of steam provides the slight amount of dampness needed to get truly flat seams or edges. Curved or softly draped sections of your garment may be "set" to hang correctly by steaming them into position. Steam is of special value for collars and lapels. They will always roll correctly if carefully steamed in position on a dress form or a rolled towel during construction.

seams

Initially, all seams are treated alike. Press along the stitching line in the same direction as the seam was sewn to merge stitches with fabric. Open the seam flat with the tip of your iron. Then let the shape of the seam dictate further handling.

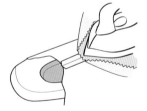

FLAT SEAMS often leave ridges in the right side of your garment. Steam press with the garment over a seam roll or with brown paper under the seam allowances.

CURVED or **ROUNDED SEAMS** pose different problems. The seamline should be pressed flat, but the seam area should maintain its built-in roundness. Employ the techniques used for a flat seam, but vary the equipment. Use a tailor's ham or dressmaker's cushion as your pressing surface.

SEAMS AT FINISHED EDGES with allowances completely enclosed within parts of your garment (such as facings, cuffs, pocket flaps, and collars) should be pressed before turning. After stitching, place the seam over the edge of a point presser or tailor's board and open it with the tip of your iron to facilitate turning and ensure a flat seam that will not roll. Next, lay the section flat on the ironing board with the underside up. Turn pressed seam allowances toward the section until the stitching line shows and press very lightly to make turning and favoring the outer edge easier. Turn right side out and press with a cloth from the underside; keep the seam on the underside.

 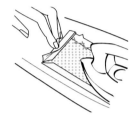 

darts

Darts require a subtly rounded pressing surface such as a tailor's ham.

First press the dart flat, as it was stitched, being careful not to let your iron stray past the pointed end. Then open the garment and press the dart in the proper direction, working from the wider end toward the point. Do not give the dart a sharp crease until the garment has been fitted. Over a rounded surface, open the dart edges with the tip of your iron. Using a press cloth, press darts completely open. After pressing the dart, press the surrounding garment area.

In general, vertical darts are pressed toward center back or front and horizontal darts are pressed downward.

Press contour or double pointed darts like single-pointed darts, one half of the dart at a time, working from the middle to the pointed ends.

Slash darts in heavy fabrics along the fold to within ½" to 1" (13mm to 25mm) of the point.

tucks

First press tucks from underneath side of fold. Retain the soft fold of a released tuck by never pressing past the stitching line. Be cautious with steam; too much may cause puckering. Press the fold of released tucks toward center front or back from wrong side. Tucks made on right side are pressed from stitching line toward folds; put brown paper under folds of wide tucks. Always use a press cloth when pressing from right side.

gathers

Press from the wrong side wherever possible. Hold the gathering along the stitching as you work. Move your iron from the flat, un-gathered area toward the rows of stitching. Use the tip of your iron to get between the folds of fabric. Repeat the procedure until no sharp creases remain. Press gathered seam allowances flat before stitching.

pleats

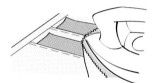

SHARP PLEATS, when you are sure of fit, baste the length of each pleat.

Press on both sides of the pleat, using a press cloth and very little steam. Press just enough to set the pleat. If the pleats fall correctly, press again to within 8" (20.5cm) of the lower edge, setting the creases permanently. Use strips of brown paper under the folds. Hem and set remainder of pleat creases. (Press the full length if the hem is already completed.) If garment is hanging off the ironing board, support with a chair or table to prevent distortion of the pleats.

SOFT or **UNPRESSED PLEATS** should be steamed gently into folds rather than sharp creases.

Place the garment on a dress form so the folds fall naturally and steam thoroughly with your iron. If a dress form is not available, pin the pleats in place on your ironing board cover and steam them, holding the iron 2" to 3" (5cm to 7.5cm) from the fabric. Let the fabric dry completely before removing the garment from the board.

plackets and zippers

Because these features can be found in curved or flat areas, let the shape of the garment area determine the appropriate equipment to use.

Position your placket right side down on a press pad, thick woolen scrap, or a heavy towel placed on your ironing board, or a tailor's ham. The padding will prevent unwanted ridges from appearing as you press. Work from the wrong side; use a press cloth and limited moisture since excess dampness may create puckers. Do not press directly on zipper teeth, hooks and eyes, or snaps to avoid marring them or the sole plate of your iron. Should you need to touch up the right side of your fabric, place brown paper between the placket lap and the fabric underneath and press, protecting the fabric with a press cloth, using limited moisture.

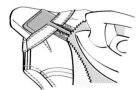

buttonholes

Since buttonholes call for detailed construction techniques, you'll find that careful pressing applied at the appropriate times will greatly simplify the entire procedure.

After stitching the buttonhole to the garment, use a press cloth and brown paper under the strip edges to press the buttonhole from the right side, merging fabric and threads. Then use a sleeve board, placing the wrong side of the buttonhole area on the larger side of the board to prevent the surrounding garment area from becoming wrinkled. Lift up the strips and touch up portions of the garment between the buttonholes, if necessary. Then lay garment flat on ironing board and press the surrounding garment area.

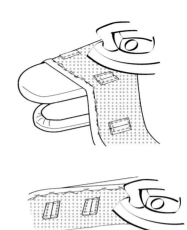

pockets

After stitching the pocket to the garment, press from the right side, using a press cloth. For welt or flap pockets, first put brown paper between the garment and the welt or flap. Then turn to the wrong side and press along seamlines, using a press pad. Then lift up the pocket and touch up the garment area underneath the pocket, using the moisture appropriate to your fabric.

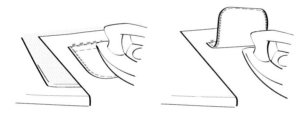

sleeves

Start by pressing the sleeve seam open over a sleeve board. After easing and fitting the sleeve cap, remove the sleeve from the garment and place it on the narrow end of a sleeve board. Then use the tip and side of your iron to shrink the fullness from the seam allowance only. Be very careful not to press beyond the stitching line or flatten the sleeve cap. Some fabrics, such as permanent press and velvet, do not respond well to shrinking. After the sleeve has been stitched into the garment, press along the seam over a tailor's ham to blend the stitches into your fabric. Avoid extending the iron into the sleeve cap and use steam sparingly.

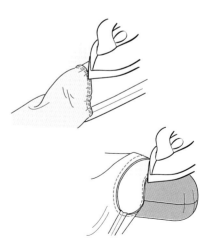

hems

After marking, baste hems near the fold. Place brown paper between hem and garment and steam out any excess fullness. Avoid pressing over basting threads. Holding the iron above the hem, steam it, shrinking out as much fullness as possible.

SHARP CREASE: Once hem has been sewn in place, remove basting. Steam again. Use a pounding block if a crisp edge is desired.

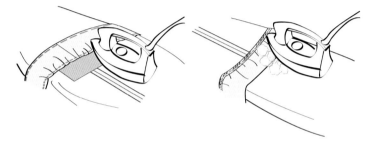

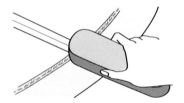

SOFT HEMS with a gently rolled edge may be preferred in place of a sharp crease. Place garment on ironing surface and hold the iron 2" to 3" (5cm to 7.5cm) from interfaced hem, steaming the fabric thoroughly. Never rest the iron directly on the fabric. Pat lightly with a pounding block or ruler to mold the hem. Let the garment dry thoroughly before wearing.

PLEATED HEMS with seams at the fold must be pressed carefully before hemming.

Clip the pleat seam at the top of the turned up hem before the raw edge is finished. Press seam allowances open below clip. Grade the seam allowances of bulky fabric. Finish the raw edge and complete the hem. Press a sharp crease in the underfold with the edge of your iron. If the folds still do not lie flat, stitch close to the edge of the fold.

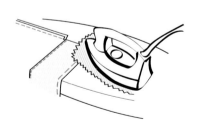

final pressing

The last pressing operation should be a mere touch-up job, never a cure-all for haphazard pressing during construction. Soft pleats, godets, collars, and other areas that need "setting" should be pressed with the garment on a dress form or hanger. Just steam and pat into position without touching your iron to the fabric. You may use tissue paper padding under collars, inside sleeve caps, and in other areas to hold them in place while the fabric dries. Do not remove your garment from dress form until the fabric is completely dry.

pattern sizing charts

Use these pattern sizing charts to find your correct pattern size.

MISSES': The Misses' size patterns are designed for a figure 5'5" to 5'6" (1.65 to 1.68M) tall without shoes, well proportioned and developed. The standard full hip measurement is 9" (23cm) below the waist.

MISSES' PETITES: A shorter figure, the Misses' Petites size patterns are for a person approximately 5'2" to 5'4" (1.57 to 1.63M) tall without shoes, and who has a back waist length 1" (2.5cm) shorter than the Misses' figure. The distance between the waist and full hip measurements is 7" (18cm). As a rule, the Misses' Petite figure also has shorter shoulder-to-elbow and elbow-to-wrist measurements.

SIZE	6	8	10	12	14	16	18	20	22	24
Chest	28½ (73)	29½ (75)	30½ (78)	32 (81)	34 (87)	36 (92)	38 (97)	40 (102)	42 (107)	44 (112)
Bust	30½ (78)	31½ (80)	32½ (83)	34 (87)	36 (92)	38 (97)	40 (102)	42 (107)	44 (112)	46 (117)
Waist	23 (58)	24 (61)	25 (64)	26½ (67)	28 (71)	30 (76)	32 (81)	34 (87)	37 (94)	39 (99)
Hip	32½ (83)	33½ (85)	34½ (88)	36 (92)	38 (97)	40 (102)	42 (107)	44 (112)	46 (117)	48 (122)
Back Waist Length	15½ (39.5)	15¾ (40)	16 (40.5)	16¼ (41.5)	16½ (42)	16¾ (42.5)	17 (43)	17¼ (44)	17½ (44.5)	17¾ (45)

WOMEN'S: The Women's figure stands 5'5" to 5'6" (1.65 to 1.68M) without shoes, but is a somewhat larger, more fully mature figure than the standard Misses' figure.

SIZE	14W	16W	18W	20W	22W	24W	26W	28W	30W	32W
	-	-	-	(38)	(40)	(42)	(44)	(46)	(48)	(50)
Bust	36	38	40	42	44	46	48	50	52	54
	(92)	(97)	(102)	(107)	(112)	(117)	(122)	(127)	(132)	(137)
Waist	29	31	33	35	37	39	41½	44	46½	49
	(73)	(78)	(84)	(89)	(94)	(99)	(105)	(112)	(118)	(124)
Hip	38	40	42	44	46	48	50	52	54	56
	(97)	(102)	(107)	(112)	(117)	(122)	(127)	(132)	(137)	(142)
Back Waist Length	16½	16¾	17	17¼	17⅜	17½	17⅝	17¾	17⅞	18
	(42)	(42.5)	(43)	(44)	(44)	(44.5)	(45)	(45)	(45.5)	(46)

Many women are a combination of two or more pattern sizes. Vogue Multi-Size patterns combine three or more sizes in one pattern. The multiple cutting lines on the pattern enable you to change the sizes at the bust, waist, or hip, according to your figure. If the Multi-Size grouping for your pattern includes the pattern size you need for differences found on the top or bottom, pattern adjustments can be kept to a minimum. Simply choose the appropriate cutting line in each fitting area. Merge the sizes by drawing new lines that gradually blend different cutting lines.

today's fit patterns

To meet the changing proportions of the American woman, a new pattern category was developed in 1999 at Vogue Patterns, called Today's Fit. Spearheaded by Sandra Betzina, syndicated sewing columnist, a new pattern sizing program was established for Vogue Patterns.

SIZE	A	B	C	D	E	F	G	H	I	J
Bust	32 (81)	34 (87)	36 (92)	38 (97)	40½ (103)	43 (109)	46 (117)	49 (124)	52 (132)	55 (140)
Waist	26½ (67)	28½ (72)	30½ (78)	32½ (83)	35 (89)	37½ (95)	41½ (105)	44½ (113)	47½ (121)	50½ (128)
Hip	34½ (88)	36½ (93)	38½ (98)	40½ (103)	42½ (108)	45 (116)	48 (122)	51 (130)	54 (137)	57 (145)
Back Waist Length	15¾ (40)	16 (40.5)	16¼ (41)	16½ (42)	16¾ (42.5)	17 (43)	17¼ (44)	17¼ (44)	17¼ (44)	17¼ (44)

index

index

Vogue Sewing Quick Reference